© 2006
YouthLight, Inc.
Chapin, SC 29036

All rights reserved.
Permission is given for individuals to reproduce pages as noted in this book.
Reproduction of any other material is strictly prohibited.

Cover Design and Layout by Amy Rule
Cover Drawing by Stephanie Jenkins
Illustrations Coordinated by Kimberly Grant
Project Editing by Susan Bowman

ISBN
1-59850-005-8

Library of Congress Number
2005930661

10 9 8 7 6 5 4 3 2 1
Printed in the United States

 Illustrators

Special Thanks to the Students at Northwestern High School in Rock Hill, South Carolina:

Lauren Arnold
Sara Boone
Jenna Cauthen
Jennifer Eubanks
Stephanie Eury
Lindsay Fincher
Amanda Gaskins
Becky Hunt
Stephanie Jenkins
Anthony Lambruschi
Sarah LeBlanc
Ashley Phaup
Cara Sicilia
Samantha St. Aubin
Christine Walton
Beth Zimmerman

About the Authors

Sue Smith-Rex, Ed.D. and James H. Rex, Ph.D. have retired with a combination of sixty-five years in both higher education and K-12 education. Sue is a retired professor of Special Education from Winthrop University in Rock Hill, South Carolina. After thirty years of teaching in both public schools and higher education, she is now doing consulting work involving "at risk" issues

and is the owner of a small business. In addition to co-authoring twelve books, she has conducted workshops throughout the United States on topics of attention deficit hyperactivity disorder and school bullying. She has been the recipient of many professional awards; 1998- South Carolina Association of Counselors' Humanitarian Award; 1992- President Bush's Point of Light Award; and the 1998- Jefferson Pilot recipient of the Jefferson Award for public service.

Jim recently retired as president of Columbia College in Columbia, South Carolina. Prior to that he was the Vice President for Institutional Advancement at the University of South Carolina, the Vice Chancellor for Academic Affairs at Coastal Carolina University, and the Dean of Education at Winthrop University and at Coastal Carolina University. Jim was also on the faculty of the University of Toledo and taught high school English and coached varsity football in Ohio.

Sue and Jim remain committed to the improvement of teaching and learning for every student in America's schools and to the unique contribution our schools continue to make to the American Dream of equal opportunity for all. The Rexes have four adult children: Jeffrey, Adam, Siri, and Nathan.

Table of Contents

Introduction: Note to Parents and Health Professionals 6

Part I: Illustrated Single-Page Insights for Students 8

*Part II: Practical Ideas That Teachers and Counselors Can
              Use to Help Create Happier Students* 42

    Evaluate Yourself and Consider Making Changes 43
    Think-Look-and-Act Assertive 44
    Who Has the Control? 45
    Chart Your Feelings! 47
    The Effects of Negative Thinking 48
    Front Burner-Back Burner Approach 49
    Setting Goals in My Life 50
    Prioritize Daily Commitments to Avoid Feeling Overwhelmed 51
    Monthly Plan Sheet 52
    Learning Self-Control – Do NOT Procrastinate 53
    What are Rational and Irrational Fears? 54
    Evaluate Your Anxiety 55
    Common Thinking Errors of Depressed Students 56
    The Friendship Model 57
    Use Positive Affirmations! 58
    Good Eye Contact, Firm Handshakes, Healthy Smile 59
    Rate Your Popular Mannerisms 60
    Reach Out and Control Isolation 62
    Selecting the Right Friends 63
    Simple Refusal Skills 64
    Memorize Assertive Phrases 65
    Dream and Reflect 66
    Gardner's Multiple Intelligence Theory 67
    Feeling and Believing You Are Good at Something 68
    Finding A Cause You Believe In 69
    Habit Forming Acts of Kindness 70

Table of Contents

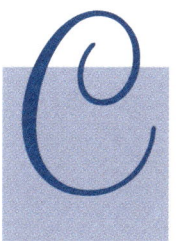

Part III: Practical Ideas to Help Your Child Grow Into a Happier Adult 72

Modeling – The Dance of Parenthood 73
Over Structuring Childhood 74
Helping Your Child Deal With Rejection 75
Parental Storytelling 76
Stick to Commitments 77
Components to a Healthy Self-Esteem 78
10 Things Parents Can Do To Help Children Develop A Healthy Self-Esteem 79
The Natural World 80
Personal Beliefs/ Spirituality 81
Knowing Your Family History and Ethnic Heritage 82
Be A Model For Your Children! 83
Coaching Your Child's Health Habits 84
Knowing When To Feel Pride Versus Gratitude 85
Learning to Aim Before We Fire! 86
Envisioning Our Futures 87
The Gift of Giving 88
Discovering Your Optimum Environment 89
Learning to Avoid "Jerks" 90
Finding the Humor in Life 91
Avoiding an Unexamined Life 92

Final Thought on "The Pursuit of Happiness" 93

References 94

Introduction

This Nation's Founding Fathers understood that the "pursuit of happiness" is an essential and universal human need. This "pursuit" is manifested in many ways throughout our culture as we enter the 21st century. The evidence of our failures and successes are everywhere. There is the increasing consumption of mood "enhancing" drugs such as Prozac. There are the millions who flock to therapists, plastic surgeons, and a variety of self-help pundits as we seek to feel, look and/or act in ways that at least portray us to be happier and more contented human beings.

We buy more, consume more, and invent more material goods as we seek ever greater satisfaction. We live longer, yet many of us reach mid life with a surprising sense of emptiness. We seek peace in our spiritual pursuits; love and security within our families; delight in our art. When asked, most of us believe that we are fortunate to live in a wealthy and privileged society, but many feel dissatisfied and disillusioned with their own lives.

There is an increasing amount of research being done on the subject of human happiness. Happiness is something we hope for throughout our lives, not only for ourselves, but also for our family and for those we care about. Happiness can mean different things to different people, but generally it means that the circumstances in one's life bring pleasure and a sense of well being.

Certainly no one can snap their fingers and be instantly and constantly happy, but researchers believe that how we look at our lives can make a real difference. An important component of happiness is feeling as if you have an acceptable level of control within your life. Much in life is a matter of perspective. A person can view something as good or bad, a success or a failure, a roadblock or a challenge. How individuals decide to look at the options and opportunities that present themselves throughout their lives can bring greater appreciation, hope, peace, and happiness. In other words, happiness is a state that can be nurtured.

Part One of this book is geared to upper elementary, middle and high school students, with supplementary artwork created by high school seniors. The descriptions, information, and recommendations are designed to enable adolescents to gain practical insights into how they can begin to exercise control over how they feel about themselves and their lives – their happiness.

The format chosen for Part One is a series of verbal and visual communications designed to gain and hold the attention of the targeted audience. However, whether you are an adolescent, or an adult, Part One will likely contain new insights for you regarding how happiness is defined, and influenced, by the decisions each of us make.

Introduction

Part Two is intended for teachers, counselors, and social workers by providing specific ideas to help students achieve greater levels of happiness. Concrete activities, techniques, and exercises are provided along with some useful handouts specifically designed to be duplicated.

Part Three is written for parents who seek assistance in nurturing the precious gift of happiness in their child. Most parents instinctively know when their child needs help. The difficulty is knowing how best to lead, support, and direct them in their personal life-quest.

Part Three contains specific and practical suggestions for parents on how they can both assist and enable their child in his or her pursuit of happiness.

Finally, whether you read every page of this book as a teacher, counselor, social worker or parent, or only Part One as an adolescent, our sincere desire is that you, your student, and/or child will benefit from the effort.

For Adolescents

Part I

Illustrated Single-Page Insights for Students

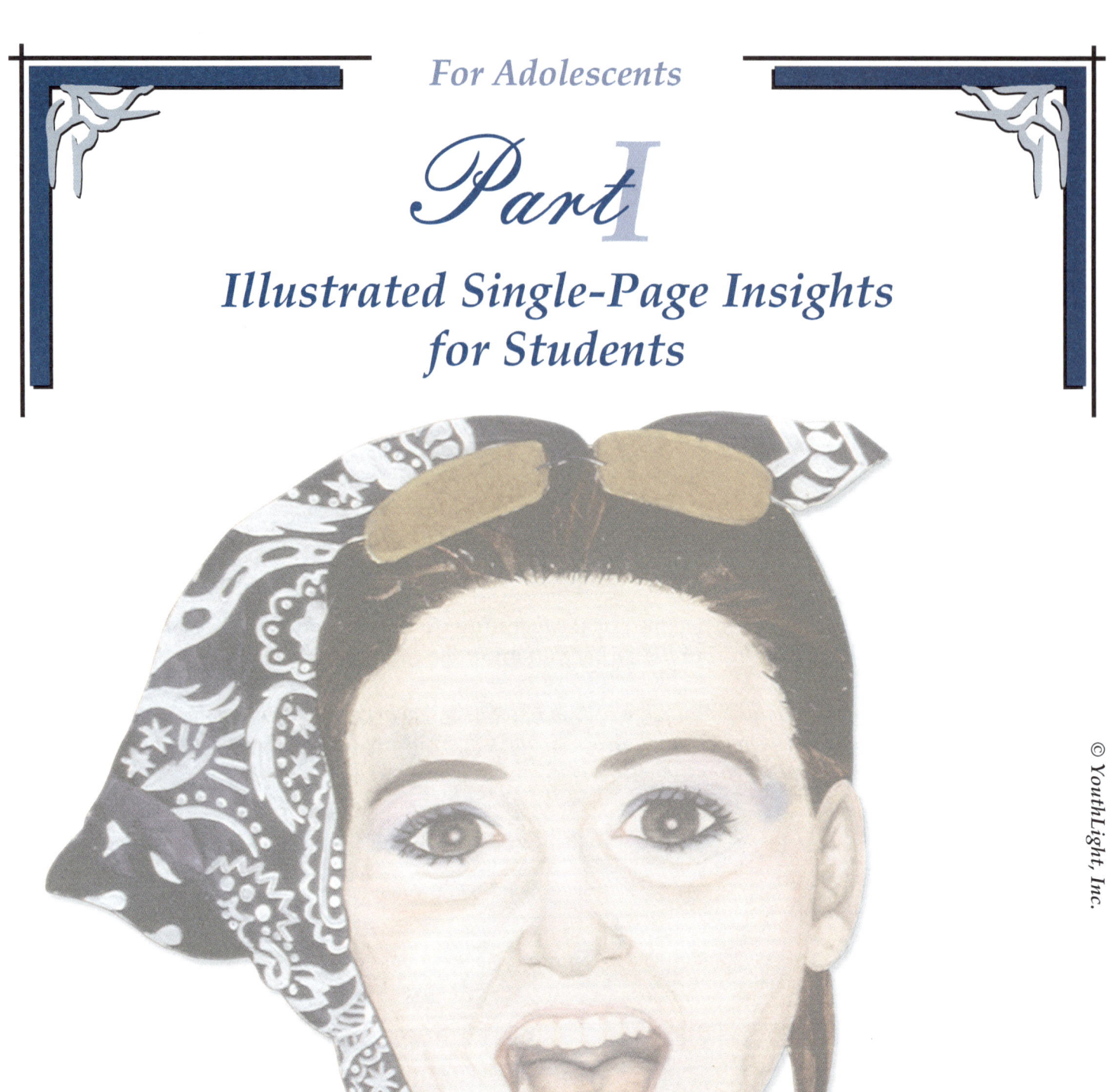

For Adolescents

Sharing the Light

Becky Hunt

Educators, philosophers, and religious leaders have thought about, written about, and spoken about the topic of happiness for centuries. More recently, researchers have began to look closely at the characteristics and assumptions that effect the human condition(s) we describe as "happiness." Happiness is something we all hope for throughout our lives, not only for ourselves, but also for our family and loved ones. Happiness means different things to different people, but generally it means that the circumstances in one's life bring personal pleasure and a sense of well being.

For Adolescents
Expectation

Jennifer Eubanks

Certainly no one can snap their fingers and be instantly and constantly happy, but researchers believe that how we look at our lives can make a real difference. This is called perception. An important component of happiness is personally feeling as if you have an acceptable level of control within your everyday life and an acceptable level of optimism about the future.

For Adolescents

Panorama

Beth Zimmerman

A person can view something as good or bad, a success or a failure, a roadblock or a challenge. It is a matter of perception. How individuals decide to look at the options and opportunities that present themselves during their lives can bring greater appreciation, hope, peace, and happiness. In other words, happiness is a state of mind that can be nurtured.

For Adolescents

Mind's Eye

Ashley Phaup

Emotions are felt by all people every day. Emotions are feelings that range from love and happiness all the way to anger, disappointment, and even hopelessness. Emotions are a normal part of life. How we react to our feelings can either be helpful or hurtful. To a large extent this choice can only be controlled by you.

For Adolescents

The Mummy

Jenna Cauthen

Although everyone will feel positive or pleasant feelings as well as negative or unpleasant feelings during life, it is important to not get "stuck" on unpleasant feelings for long periods of time. This can lead to depression, a serious illness, which can prevent individuals from enjoying the beauty of life.

For Adolescents

Blue Genes

Lindsay *Fincher*

© *YouthLight, Inc.*

O ne of the biggest questions addressed in more recent research is how much control do individuals have over their feelings of happiness. It is believed that about half of a person's basic satisfaction comes from our biological genes (Lykken, 1996). If parents are usually in good moods and basically happy people, this increases our chances of being genetically programmed to feel the same way more often.

For Adolescents

Jellin

Sara Boone

Everyone is born with a basic range of happiness potential. Some individuals are inclined to be happy and optimistic and others are inclined to be sad and pessimistic. However, it is important to know that 96% of individuals surveyed rated their satisfaction with life as "fairly" positive (Diener & Diener, 1996). In other words, most people are not happy all of the time, so there is nothing unusual about having some sad feelings as long as sadness does not dominate your emotions.

For Adolescents

Synergy

Lauren Arnold

There are over 60 brain chemicals that serve different functions. There are 3 main chemicals which help to regulate how happy we feel. The first one is dopamine, which bathes neurons involved in memory and emotion. With more dopamine more neurons are activated, reinforcing feelings of joy. The second chemical is endorphins, which promotes pleasure by dampening pain and producing a feeling of well being. The third chemical is seretonin. Low levels of this chemical tends to produce feelings of depression. The level of these chemicals are for the most part genetically programmed. However, chemical imbalances can often be treated and kept from interfering with our potential for feeling happiness (Time, 1/17/05, p.A14).

For Adolescents
Face-Off

Cara Sicilia

The Harvard's School of Public Health did a study which reported that the people who rank in the upper ranges of happiness develop 50% more antibodies than the average person in response to flu vaccines, and therefore have a lower risk of death. People who are frequently unhappy and often fearful release a higher level of the brain chemical cortisol, which can decrease the T-cells produced by the body, which fight disease and infections (Time, 1/17/05, p.A12).

For Adolescents

Clear View

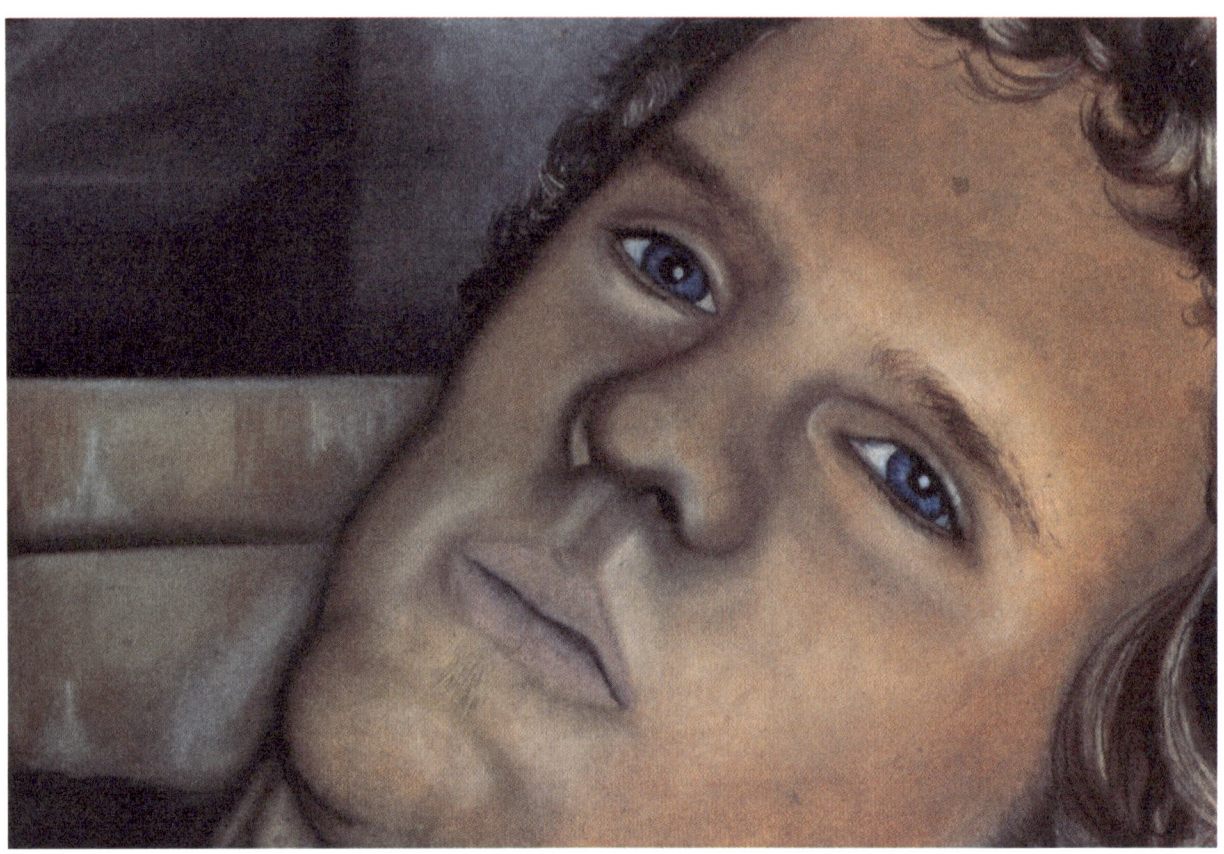

Cara Sicilia

Sporadic doses of negative experiences are inevitable in life and can be valuable. It is through stressful events that people learn to bounce back from unpleasant emotions. This ability is often referred to as resiliency. Why are some children able to endure extreme circumstances such as poverty, a parent's absence, and a violent neighborhood – and yet bounce back from adversity better than "privileged" children who are defeated by the mildest setbacks? No one really knows, but it is certain that learning from adversity and increasing your level of resiliency should also increase your chances for happiness.

For Adolescents
Holding On

Becky Hunt

There are specific things young people can do to help themselves grow up to be happy individuals. For example, there appear to be a number of characteristics and activities, often associated with resiliency, that can improve all of our odds for achieving happiness.

The one thing you can do to increase your chances of achieving happiness is to find a cause you believe in and give of yourself in terms of your time and energy. When a person becomes engaged in a project it gives one's life additional meaning and often brings personal pleasure. Some examples of causes are projects at school, church, and neighborhoods or even to help improve conditions at the state or national level.

For Adolescents
Girlfriend

Beth Zimmerman

Individuals who learn how to be a good friend are often more positively engaged at school, at home, and in their community. People who have friends are more likely to feel a sense of happiness. Some of the skills anyone can learn, which can lead to new friendships are listed below.

- *Make it a habit to smile often!*
- *Do not wish bad things for others.*
- *Use positive statements.*
- *Do not act jealous of those who are doing well.*
- *Say nice things about other people.*
- *Talk to people first and ask how they are doing.*
- *Reach out to help someone else.*
- *Talk often to people who make up your support team.*
- *Realize and accept that some things are out of your control.*

For Adolescents
"Cheese"

Lauren Arnold

Happiness is enhanced by a good sense of humor. Laughter tends to reduce the production of the stress hormone cortisol (Time, 1/17/05, p.A17). Laughter is something we seldom do alone. Humor is fun to be around, so having this personal characteristic increases the chances of friendships developing.

For Adolescents

The Possible

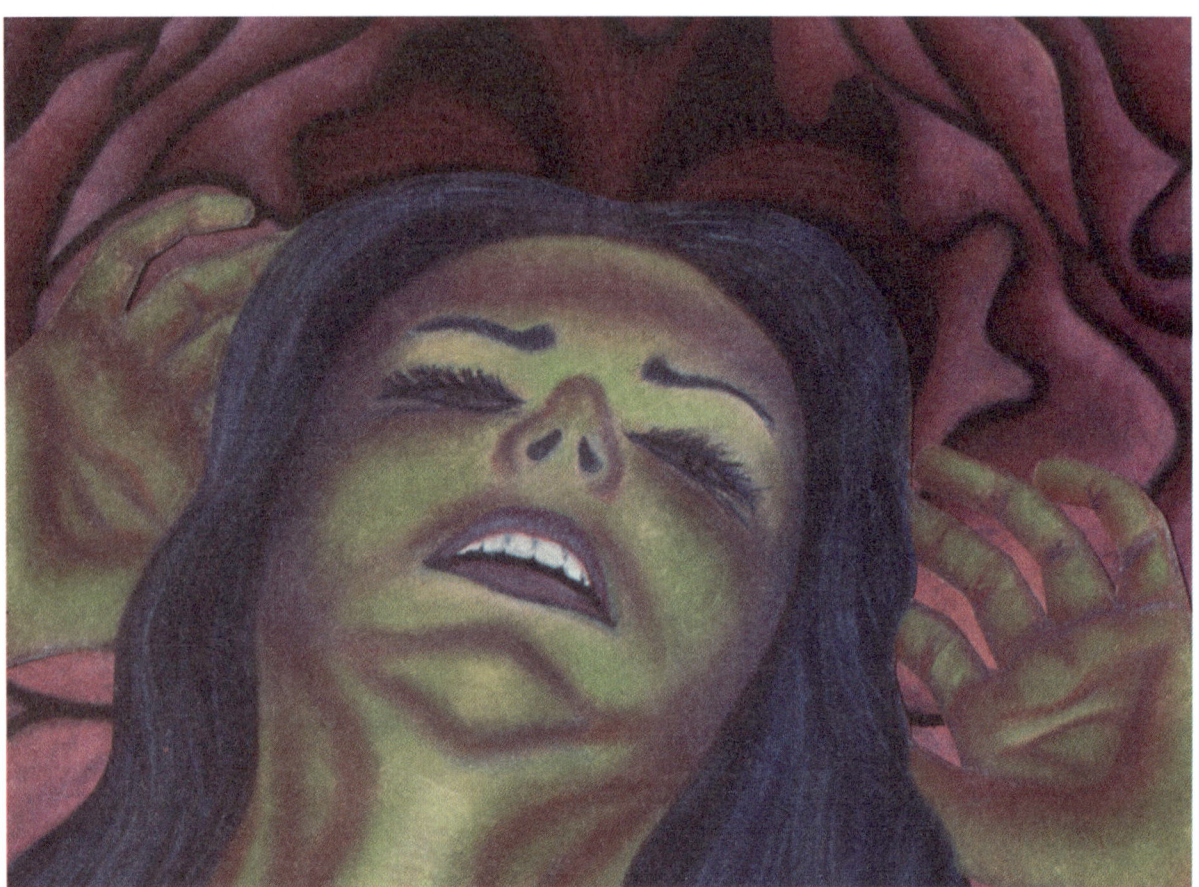

Christine Walton

© YouthLight, Inc.

Individuals with an "internal locus of control" feel confident that they can make good decisions in life. This personal quality helps people to become more self-motivated. It is important for students that parents and teachers help them acquire the skills necessary to make intelligent and moral decisions throughout their lives.

For Adolescents

Sun Dial

Amanda Gaskins

Individuals who learn to consistently use positive, assertive phrases when describing their decisions and/or their needs, are likely to be listened to by others and to, therefore, have influence over others. Having the confidence to use positive, assertive phrases helps individuals see life and its changing condition as less overwhelming and more manageable. In part II of this book, we will describe a few phrases that your counselor, teacher, or parent can practice with you to help you feel more confident using.

For Adolescents

Pole Cats

Ashley *Phaup*

Many people add to their level of happiness by appreciating and understanding our natural environment. Individuals who have opportunities to learn about and appreciate nature's beauty are more likely to appreciate the beauty of all life and to participate in activities that enable one to tap into the wonder and awe of the natural world around them. Sometimes when a person is outdoors enjoying fresh air and beautiful surroundings it helps to put disappointments in perspective and to sense the "bigger picture" that goes beyond their more limited, personal concerns.

For Adolescents

Rose Colored

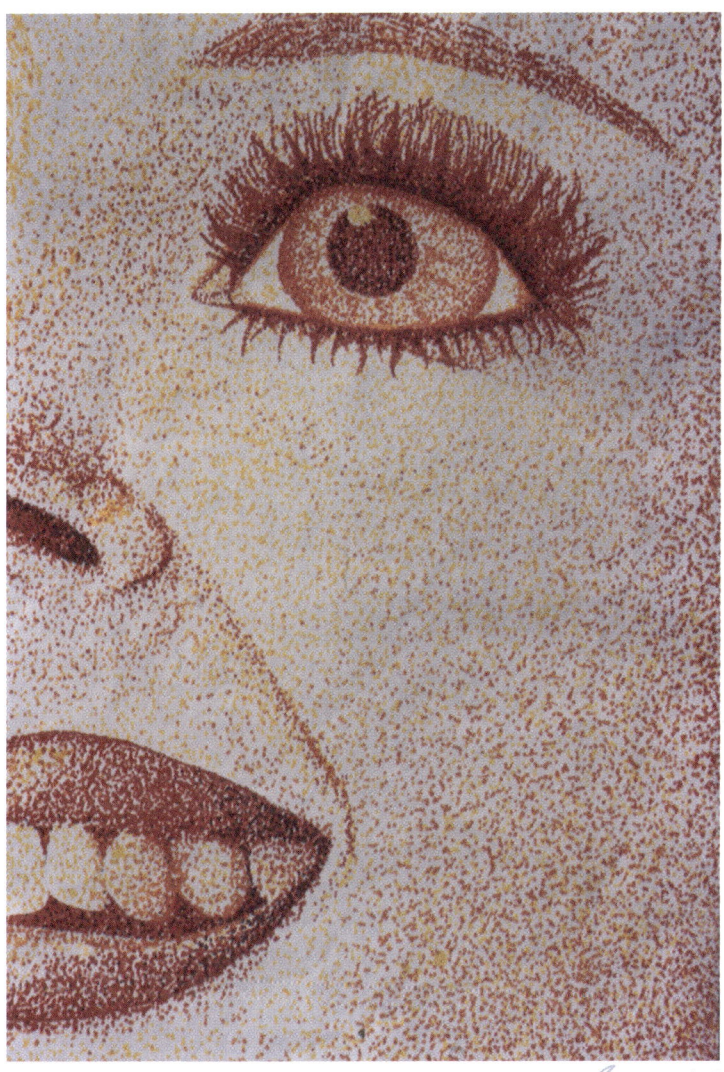

Lauren *Arnold*

Happiness is more likely when people have a positive view of the future. Individuals who have a sense of hope regarding the future tend to be both optimistic and happier. This is more likely to happen when children grow up around optimistic, positive adults and when homes and schools conspire to support children and ensure that they feel competent and significant.

It is good to try to surround yourself with positive, moral individuals. The selection of your friends is something that one can control.

For Adolescents

Believin

Sarah LeBlanc

Kids who are resilient have often found "something" to be better at than the average person. Often we think just of academics or sports but it can be any hobby, skill, or knowledge area. With the proper efforts and opportunities, virtually every child can find an area within which he or she can excel. Feeling and believing you are good at something can raise the odds of achieving personal happiness.

For Adolescents

Champs

Ashley Phaup

Everyone deserves to have a personal champion. Sometimes they come to us and sometimes we must go to them. Strong mentors, which can be parents, teachers, clergy, coaches, relatives or friends, provide important support. Strong champions or role models help kids learn how to achieve a feeling of success by believing in themselves and developing a strong self-esteem. Positive thinking is important to our good health and happiness. It allows us to set goals and gives us hope that our efforts will pay off. Sometimes a champion can help us to more easily realize our potential.

For Adolescents

Hollow

Lindsay Fincher

Individuals who are consistently unhappy sometimes abandon their peers who are thinking positive thoughts and making good moral decisions in favor of new peers who are also unhappy and making poor choices. Sometimes, "misery really does love company," but it almost never brings about improvement. In fact, this can lead to a very destructive pattern of behavior that can lead to hurtful consequences for yourself, your family, and your community.

For Adolescents

Life Lines

Cara Sicilia

An important quality that brings happiness to many people is a personal faith in something greater than oneself. Religious and spiritual people tend to be less depressed and have a greater sense of well-being. A personal faith can support four major benefits: social support, spiritual support, a sense of purpose, and boundaries to assist in making more thoughtful daily choices and behavioral decisions (Time, 1/17/05, p.A46).

For Adolescents

Split Decision

Ashley *Phaup*

Happiness is largely generated by one's personal accomplishments. Be grateful for what you have, materialistic and non-materialistic, and build upon your base. Imagine for a moment that today is your last day on Earth. If you made a list of the important things you feel you have accomplished, are proud of, or that make you happy, what would be on your list? Probably not your material possessions! Remember where you started and appreciate how much you have accomplished. Know your family history and ethnic heritage. This will offer many people a sense of pride and purpose.

For Adolescents

See the Point

Sarah LeBlanc

Although it is normal to get bored with day to day chores and commitments, happy people tend to set realistic goals and are disciplined about coping with life's chores, setting up a daily routine, not procrastinating and not complaining about what needs to be done. Sometimes, the busiest people seem to also be among the happiest. If you look closely, they often have habits and skills that enable them to not be overwhelmed by a life that is full and satisfying.

For Adolescents

Just Doing It!

Ashley *Phaup*

Research on physical activity finds that exercise increases self-confidence (Fontane, 1996). Virtually everyone, with discipline, can get into the habit of exercising on a regular basis each week. Exercise also generates the production of the brain chemicals dopamine, seretonin, and endorphins, which can act as mood enhancers.

For Adolescents

Lovefest

Christine Walton

Those who have a loved pet are 22% more likely to feel satisfied than those without pets. Science can't fully explain the power of loving a pet, but numerous studies have shown that animals can help lower blood pressure and cholesterol levels, raise survival after a heart attack, and reduce loneliness and depression (Barofsky & Rowan, 1998).

For Adolescents
Major Rose

Stephanie Eury

A positive effect on mood was found for 92% of individuals when they listened to the music of their choice. Music often leads to reflection of happy times and events. Scientists have found that music stimulates our brain and adds to our sense of well-being (Hakanen, 1995).

For Adolescents
Groovin

Sarah LeBlanc

If you don't have a hobby, get one! Hobbies can add fun and consistency to an individual's life. It is something you can share with family and friends, and it is something that can help you feel skillful and productive.

For Adolescents
Tuned Out

Christine Walton

Make sure you are taking care of your body by getting enough sleep throughout each week and eating healthy foods. One study reported that every hour of sleep sacrificed results in an 8% less positive feeling about the following day (Pitcher & Ott, 1998). Usually we can get enough sleep if we use our time wisely and have the discipline to turn off the TV and computer and limit our use of the phone.

A Pair

Cara Sicilia

Another study associated healthy eating with consuming enough fruit. Eating more fruit is likely to create an 11% higher likelihood of feeling capable and satisfied. Individuals became less interested in eating junk food and ultimately packing on the pounds (Heatey & Thombs, 1997).

For Adolescents

Petal Mettle

Becky Hunt

Just as our sense of hearing is stimulated by music, and our sense of taste is stimulated by fruit, our sense of smell is stimulated by pleasant aromas. Unpleasant aromas trigger unhappy thoughts and pleasant smells evoke pleasant thoughts. One simple way to increase a feeling of pleasure is to air out our living space and add some fragrant effects.

For Adolescents

Silent Bleachers

Beth Zimmerman

People have always derived happiness from supporting their athletic teams, whether it is middle school, high school, college teams, professional teams, male or female. Actively supporting a local sports team was found to have positive effects by providing a common interest with others in the school or community and increasing a sense of "belonging."

For Adolescents

Trio

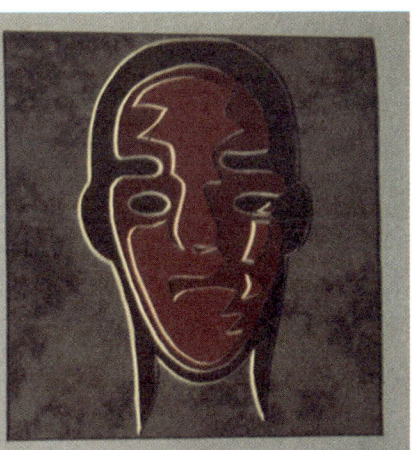

Anthony *Lambruschi*

With jobs scattering family members across the country, it takes effort to stay close to your family. Be interested in and stay involved in the lives of those you love and care about by writing, calling, and if possible visiting on a regular basis. These connections build a strong support system and often strengthen one's level of happiness.

For Adolescents

Dove Love

Christine Walton

Having the desire to display simple acts of kindness, such as holding a door open for someone, letting someone in front of you in line, visiting a neighbor, and learning to be consistently respectful, are easy ways to feel good about ourselves. Take the time and invest the energy to do simple acts of kindness for others. Others will think positively about you and you will feel good about yourself.

For Adolescents

Non Cents

Christine Walton

These suggestions should give you a framework to use when evaluating ways to increase your level of happiness. It should be quite apparent from these suggestions that money is not the answer to happiness. Therefore, happiness is something that everyone can aspire to. It is important to always believe that you are not finished with the best part of your life. This philosophy will give you a sense of hope and a motivation to continue to make the very most out of the days that lie before you.

Teachers, Counselors & Social Workers

Part II

Practical Ideas That Teachers, Counselors and Social Workers Can Use to Help Create Happier Students

42

Reproducible Worksheet

Evaluate Yourself and Consider Making Changes

Listed below are the 25 suggestions outlined in Part I of this book on nurturing individual degrees of happiness. Go down the checklist and mark the behaviors which you feel you use to your advantage. For those behaviors which you did NOT check, consider making some changes which could enhance your feelings of happiness.

- ❏ I look at most options and opportunities as a challenge rather than a roadblock.
- ❏ I view myself as a positive individual.
- ❏ I feel I have control over my anger.
- ❏ I rate my health as usually good.
- ❏ I am involved in a community or school project to help others.
- ❏ I consider myself a good friend.
- ❏ I have a good sense of humor.
- ❏ I am confident that I can make good decisions in my life.
- ❏ I appreciate and am interested in the natural environment.
- ❏ I try hard to be around positive, moral individuals.
- ❏ I have a hobby I am good at.
- ❏ I can name someone who is a personal champion for me.
- ❏ I have a personal faith in something greater than myself.
- ❏ I am knowledgeable and proud of my family and ethnic heritage.
- ❏ I do not procrastinate on a regular basis.
- ❏ I try to get regular exercise.
- ❏ I have a pet that I love.
- ❏ I enjoy listening to music.
- ❏ I try to get 8 hours of sleep each night.
- ❏ I enjoy eating fruit.
- ❏ I enjoy pleasant aromas in my home.
- ❏ I enjoy playing or cheering for my school athletic teams.
- ❏ I take the time to talk to my family and let them know I care about them.
- ❏ I use my smile frequently.
- ❏ I have a sense of hope about my future.

Teachers, Counselors & Social Workers

Think-Look-and-Act Assertive

Being assertive is a wonderful personal quality to have. Review with your students the following statements and encourage students to take time each day to reinforce their personal beliefs and skills.

Being assertive means acting confident and letting others know your feelings in positive ways. Being assertive is very different from being aggressive. Aggressive behavior is letting others know your feelings in negative ways. By displaying assertiveness skills, individuals are more likely to have a healthy self-esteem and often have a feeling of peace and well-being. There are things you can do to be considered assertive. You can think-look-and-act assertive!!

Keep calm and cool! Watch your body language. Your body language sends out important signals about how you are feeling.

To THINK assertively a person must use positive self-talk. Practice statements such as:

> I am capable.
> I am respected.
> I try to make mature choices.

To LOOK-and-ACT assertive:

> Keep your head up.
> Speak up.
> Look at the person you are talking to.
> Smile!

Teachers, Counselors & Social Workers

Who Has The Control?

Remember the only person you can control is yourself. It is impossible to change others, but you can always strive to be the best person you can be.

Review the following flowchart with your students, emphasizing that the choice to behave certain ways is up to the individual student. Then, have each student complete the worksheet on the following page.

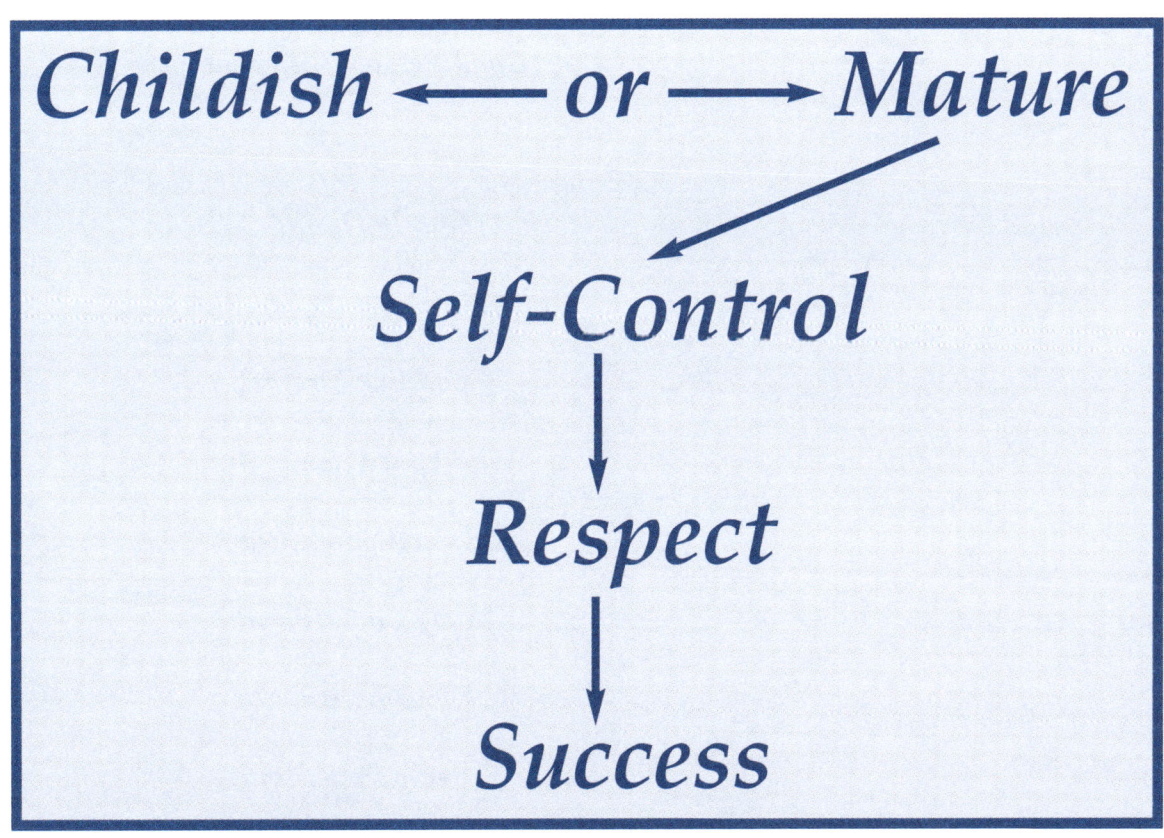

Reproducible Worksheet

Who Has The Control?

Listed below are a list of behaviors and/or responsibilities. Place a checkmark in the "Have Control" column beside those items which represent behaviors of which you have control. Place a checkmark in the "No Control" column beside those items which you do not have control. Keep working on yourself and you will find that good friendships and school success will follow.

Have Control	No Control	Behaviors / Responsibilites
		A Friendly Smile
		Crime in the Neighborhood
		Attending School Regularly
		Good Personal Hygiene
		Grades
		Family Divorce
		Hurtful Behaviors by Others
		Good Eye Contact
		Who Your Friends Are
		A Friend Shoplifting
		Giving Compliments
		Your Attitude
		Being Punctual
		The School You Attend

© YouthLight, Inc.

Reproducible Worksheet

Chart YOUR Feelings!

Write the letter of your strongest feeling three times a day for one week. Add up how often each feeling occurred and place the total in the blank space below. Which feelings occur most often? When it comes to feelings, people have pleasant feelings and they have unpleasant feelings. Everyone experiences both types during life but it is important to recognize the different types and not get "stuck" on unpleasant feelings for long periods of time. Below is a list of examples of both types of feelings.

	Pleasant Feelings	# of times/wk		Unpleasant Feelings	# of times/wk
A	Happy		G	Sad	
B	Excited		H	Mad	
C	Loved		I	Frustrated	
D	Hopeful		J	Disappointed	
E	Confident		K	Embarrassed	
F	Peaceful		L	Worried	

For one entire week, using the chart below, take a minute in the morning, after school, and before bed to identify your strongest feeling. Pick a feeling word from the list above and put the letter in the appropriate box on the chart below. At the end of the week, add up how often each letter or feeling occurred and mark the total in the blank above. By charting your feelings you get to know your own personality better, and you know which emotions you need to concentrate on improving.

	Monday	Tuesday	Wednesday	Thursday	Friday	Saturday	Sunday
Morning							
Afternoon							
Evening							

Adapted from Frank, T. and Smith-Rex. S. (1995). Getting a life of your own. Minn. MN: Educational Media.

© YouthLight, Inc.

Teachers, Counselors & Social Workers

The Effects of *Negative Thinking*

Negative thinking, no matter what age, is a destructive waste of energy. The person who gets "stuck" in a cycle of negative thinking will often show some of the following signs:

1. *You have low energy levels.*
2. *You have little interest in most activities.*
3. *You can't concentrate in school.*
4. *You feel worthless.*
5. *You say things and do things you don't really mean.*
6. *You have more headaches than normal.*
7. *Your stomach or throat feels tied up like a knot.*
8. *You can't sleep well or you sleep too much.*
9. *You lose or gain too much weight.*
10. *You don't want to be around others.*

Discuss these signs with your students to get everyone to consider the following "Front Burner - Back Burner" Strategy.

Front Burner - Back Burner *Strategy*

Ask the students to think about and write down on a piece of paper all of the things that are presently worrying them. Using the "Front Burner – Back Burner" drawing, which follows, have the students write the things from their lists that they do NOT have control over on the "back burners." Then, write those things they DO have control over on the "front burners." This activity is helpful for students to concretely remove guilt over not fixing the "back burner" items and gives the students a less overwhelming feeling to be able to focus on the "front burner" items. After completing the activity, revisit the signs of negative thinking, above, and talk about ways to change negative thinking to positive thinking.

Reproducible Worksheet

Front Burner - Back Burner
Strategy

Think about and write down on a piece of paper all of the things that are presently worrying you. Using this "Front Burner – Back Burner" drawing, write the things from the list that you do NOT have control over on the "back burners." Write those things you DO have control over on the "front burners."

Back Burners

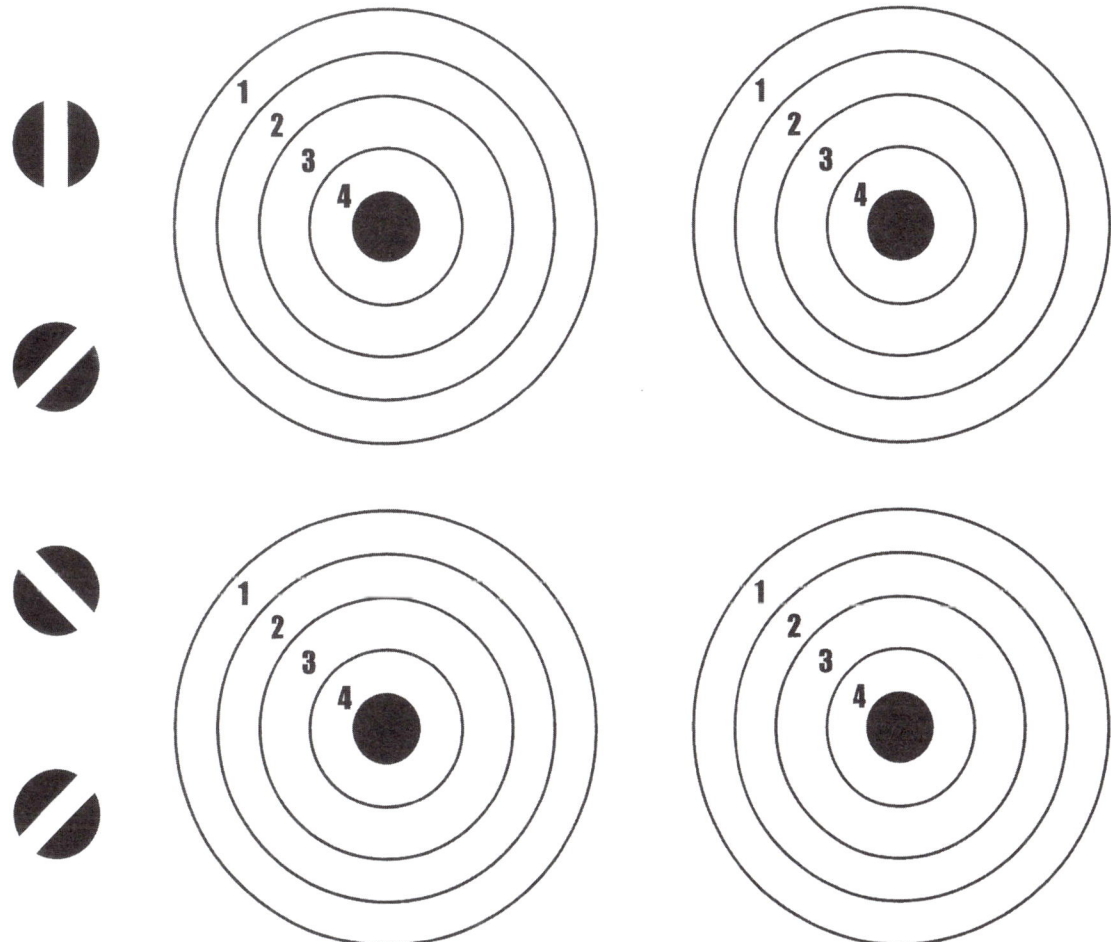

Front Burners

Adapted from Frank, T. and Smith-Rex, S. (1996). *Getting over the blues*. Minn. MN: Educational Media.

Reproducible Worksheet

Setting Goals
In My Life!

It is important, as you get older, to get into the habit of setting goals for yourself. There are short-term goals, which can be achieved during the day or week, and there are long-term goals, which may take a year or a decade to complete.

Complete the activity below by listing important, personal short-term goals in the Present File Cabinet, and listing long-term goals in the Future File Cabinet. Goals should be evaluated on a regular basis to insure that time and energy are being utilized wisely.

Present File Cabinet

Examples of short-term goals:

Study for my history test.

Finish my English paper.

Mow the grass.

Clean my room.

Future File Cabinet

Examples of long-term goals:

Complete the semester with all B's.

Be a strong member of my team.

Be selected to the honor society.

Continue to plan for college.

Teachers, Counselors & Social Workers

Prioritize Daily Commitments to Avoid Feeling Overwhelmed

Feeling overwhelmed with daily commitments can contribute to low achievement for students, anger, and possible depression. Setting and achieving goals takes daily effort. Although teachers need to introduce and practice the strategies used in this book, it is ultimately the student's responsibility to "put into action" the tools that need to be used on a consistent basis. Listed below are a few suggestions which can save time and make goals seem less overwhelming.

Lindsay Fincher

1. Turn off the television and you can gain more than 30 hours a week.

2. Don't overload yourself. Learn to say no to activities that are not important.

3. Get plenty of sleep. Fatigue can reduce your ability to deal with stress.

4. Seek out friends who inspire you and make you smile.

5. Eat a healthy diet.

6. Get regular exercise. Your body produces endorphins, a natural substance that can deliver a feeling of peacefulness.

7. Practice breathing exercises to relax your body and help you to think positively.

8. Hold your tongue! Before you place blame, count to ten. Do whatever it takes to avoid lashing out at someone.

9. Plan for free time. Block it out on your calendar just as you would an important appointment.

10. Use daily plan sheets to help you stay more organized.

Reproducible Worksheet

Monthly
Planning Sheet

Fill in the dates for the current month. Write in the box all commitments and assignments.

Monday	Tuesday	Wednesday	Thursday	Friday	Sat/Sun
___	___	___	___	___	___
___	___	___	___	___	___
___	___	___	___	___	___
___	___	___	___	___	___
___	___	___	___	___	___

© YouthLight, Inc.

Teachers, Counselors & Social Workers

Learning Self-Control
Do Not Procrastinate!

One word that describes many unmotivated, and often unhappy learners is PROCRASTINATION. When a person continually puts off requests, assignments, or duties, it allows others to look more deserving of recognition and respect.

Discuss the word PROCRASTINATION with your students and refer them back to their personal goals. One way to help students to achieve a more successful routine is to self-monitor one's behavior. By using personal prescriptions, such as the examples below, and placing them in locations that are often seen, it reminds students what needs to be accomplished. Ask students to write up personal prescriptions for home and school, but remind them it is the student's responsibility to control their own behavior.

1. Am I using good eye contact?
2. Am I speaking up?
3. Am I smiling often?
4. Are my friends right for me?

---

1. Am I in control of my anger?
2. Do I make good decisions in my life?
3. Do I procrastinate?
4. Do I have a sense of hope about the future?

---

1. Do I have a good sense of humor?
2. Do I have a personal champion in my life?
3. Do I let my family know I care about them?
4. Do I have a personal faith in something greater than myself?

Teachers, Counselors & Social Workers

What Are Rational and *Irrational Fears*

A feeling of happiness and peace is related to feeling in control of one's life. We all deal with fearful situations at some point throughout life, but the key is to understand our fears and recognize that some fears are rational and are based on reality, and some fears are irrational and can actually be controlled.

Listed below are some of the main fears that young people have identified as causing stress and sadness. Review these with your students and ask them to identify others.

- Speaking in front of class
- Bullying
- Taking tests
- Getting a bad grade
- Losing
- Violence
- Divorce
- Moving
- Changing schools
- Trying new things
- Strangers
- Storms
- Doctor visits
- Bugs or animals

It is important to be able to name our fears and consider ways to either confront our fears or learn ways to comfortably accommodate them. Rational fears are fears that might happen to anyone. Most people might become anxious if faced with the same situation. Irrational fears are less common fears and often have a distorted perception. It is helpful to ask yourself what proof there is that your perception is accurate or real. When you do this, you are using a strategy called "reality checking." When faced with an irrational fear, ask yourself the question "Is this fear something that could really hurt me?" If so, "How could I be hurt?"

When an exaggerated perception gets out of control it is called a phobia. Phobias can be so intense that they interfere with being socially accepted. A strong, healthy self-esteem is based on feeling accepted. Phobias can stand in a person's way when it comes to liking ourselves, enjoying life, or reaching one's potential.

A person can accommodate a fear by avoiding the person, thing, or event; or you can learn to confront a fear. The only way to confront a fear is to look honestly at the true risks involved and then decide how to minimize or avoid the risks without having to avoid what you fear. There is no reason to be hampered by fears. Students can often tackle fears by facing them, evaluating them, and taking control of them.

© YouthLight, Inc.

Reproducible Worksheet

Evaluate Your *Anxiety*

Anxiety is defined as: a feeling of fearful uneasiness or worry about what may happen. The following form will help you think about your fears and anxieties.

Anonymously fill out the form. If this evaluation helps you to realize that you are seeking help, let your teacher, counselor or social worker know. School help is available, but it is important for you to be your own advocate for help. Just talking about fears, hopes, goals, and strategies can make a big difference in one's life.

Do I have trouble concentrating?	Yes	No
Do I have trouble sleeping too much or too little?	Yes	No
Do I eat too much or too little?	Yes	No
Do I have a loss of interest or pleasure in doing usual activities?	Yes	No
Do I often think bad thoughts about myself?	Yes	No
Am I often in a bad mood?	Yes	No
Do I often feel a loss of energy?	Yes	No
Do I often complain about physical problems?	Yes	No
Do I often experience physical changes (heart racing, stomach upset)?	Yes	No
Do I fear certain situations and avoid them at all costs?	Yes	No
Do I recognize that others don't fear things like me?	Yes	No
Do I ever think about suicide?	Yes	No

© YouthLight, Inc.

Teachers, Counselors & Social Workers

Common Thinking Errors of Depressed Students

Teachers, counselors and social workers should provide a follow-up discussion of some of the common thinking errors of depressed students. By thinking about these errors, students may be able to take more responsibility for directing their thinking in a more positive direction. Discuss each error and ask them to come up with examples.

Stephanie Eury

Magnifying problems:
When students make things look bigger than they really are.

Jumping to conclusions:
When students consistently think the worst will happen.

"All or nothing" thinking:
When students think things are really great or really terrible.

"Taking things personally" thinking:
When students take responsibility for things that happened which may have been out of their control.

Reproducible Worksheet

The Friendship Model

Try to remember this four-step friendship model. Think about each step every time you are trying to make and keep your friends.

Check It Out

*Stop muddy messages.
Use clear messages.
Look for what you
have in common.*

Reach Out

*Give a compliment.
Use opening statements.*

Try It Out

*Talk to yourself.
Does it feel right?
Is this working?
Is it worth the effort?*

Work It Out

*Be sensitive to others.
Be trustworthy.
Be patient.
Think before acting.*

Not Working

Take a "time out."

Source: Smith, S.J. and Walter, G. *Four Steps to Making Friends*. Rock Hill, S.C.: Winthrop University.

Teachers, Counselors & Social Workers

Use Positive Affirmations!!

To affirm means to declare that something is true. The statements that people make about themselves are called affirmations. Self-talk can have a huge impact on one's consciousness. It is very important to learn how to self-monitor statements about oneself so that students, as well as others, will believe that with practice and hard work anything is possible.

Using positive affirmations regularly usually becomes a life-long habit. Other people enjoy being around individuals who are positive, upbeat and happy. When individuals give off "clear, positive messages" versus "muddy, negative messages" it greatly boosts one's popularity and hopefully their feelings of happiness. Therefore, it is important that teachers and counselors discuss the value of using positive affirmations and ask students to come up with several statements that are age appropriate.

"I use my smile a lot."

"I want to do some volunteer work."

"I will make good decisions."

"I will not procrastinate."

"I have some good friends."

Have students list and practice using their own positive affirmations. Remind students to be thankful for the good things in their lives when feeling sad or confused. One thing to keep in mind is that very few people or families are perfect. Feeling sad all the time is unproductive and will damage self-esteem.

© YouthLight, Inc.

Teachers, Counselors & Social Workers

Good Eye Contact, a Firm Handshake, and a Healthy Smile!!

All individuals are born with some tools which we can choose to use or not to use. Individuals who practice looking people in the eyes when talking to them, who reach out to say hello with a firm handshake, and use their smile often are more likely to have others admire them and enjoy being around them. These tools are used more effectively by individuals who understand their importance and practice utilizing them consistently. Just like most things, practice makes perfect!

Encourage students to use a mirror in their bedroom or bathroom to look themselves in the eyes, smile at themselves, and assertively make positive statements. Discuss the importance of speaking clearly, speaking up, and watching the tone of their voice. These assertiveness skills are admired by our society, and by displaying these skills, others see these individuals as leaders.

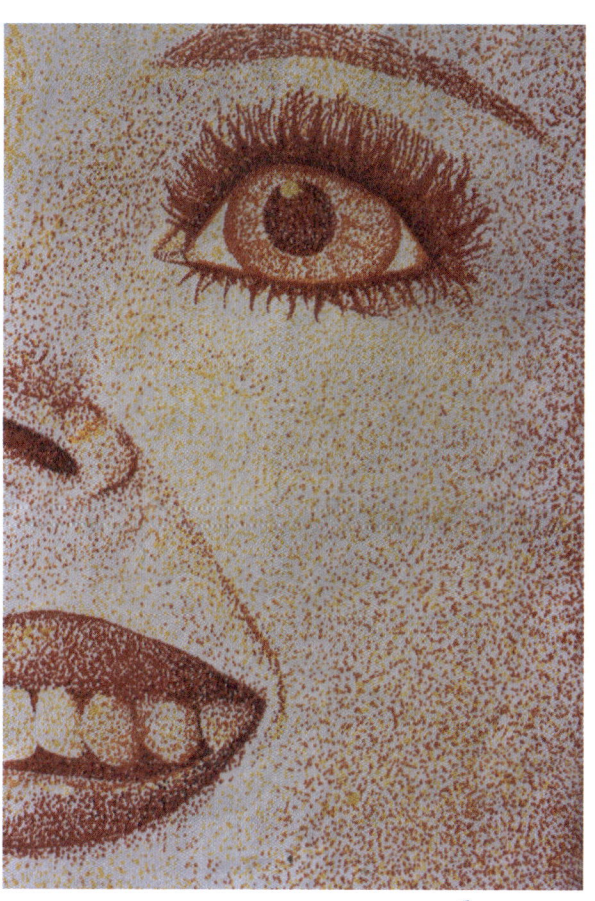

Lauren Arnold

Teachers, Counselors & Social Workers

Rate Your Popular *Mannerisms*

Some students have mannerisms that tell others they are happy, likeable, and deserving students. Listed below are some of the positive mannerisms that make some individuals more accepted, respected, and successful. Discuss these traits and then have each student rate themselves on the following scale.

Positive Mannerisms:

Do smile often.

Do use positive self-talk and affirmations.

Do not act jealous of fellow classmates who are doing well. You can do it too!!

Identify your personal champions and talk about issues.

Do what is expected of you on time and without complaining.

Reach out to others through your talk and through your time.

Remember that things on your "back burners" are out of your control. Focus your energy on things on your "front burners."

Reproducible Worksheet

Rate Your Popular *Mannerisms*

Place an "X" in the box that best describes you.

Mannerisms	Strong	OK	Poor
I smile a lot.			
I use positive affirmations.			
I say nice things about others.			
I talk to my personal champions.			
I do not regularly procrastinate.			
I like to help others.			
I focus on my "front burner" needs.			

© YouthLight, Inc.

Teachers, Counselors & Social Workers

Reach Out and *Control Isolation*

> *"Loneliness and the feeling of being unwanted is the most terrible poverty."* ~Mother Teresa

Usually the more friends we have and the busier we are, the less likely we are to feel lonely and unhappy with life. It is through discussion and reflection of this philosophy that we build EMPATHY. Use class opportunities to discuss how lonely individuals feel when they are not included. Encourage students to use and practice the skills that have been discussed earlier in the book.

1. *The Friendship Model*
2. *Good Eye Contact, a Firm Handshake and a Healthy Smile*
3. *Popular Mannerisms*

Teachers also play an important role in combating student isolation. The teacher has the power to assign status and credibility to individuals through verbal and nonverbal behaviors. By ignoring a student or reacting negatively, verbally or nonverbally, the teacher can assign a negative status to a student that can strengthen and perpetuate the isolation of that student. Look for opportunities for leadership role assignments for isolated students. Encourage social and team interactions with other students through cooperative learning and experiential learning activities. A teacher or counselor can do a lot to help a student overcome or lessen the negative effects of a poor self-concept or feelings of unhappiness.

Jenna Cauthan

© YouthLight, Inc.

Selecting the Right Friends

The Friendship Model attempts to put in outline form the four important steps to making friends and keeping friends. It is important to have many friends throughout life and to not ever limit yourself to a small clique.

Step 1

Remember to "check out" yourself so you are giving off clear messages. Others don't enjoy being around a negative individual.

Step 2

"Reach out" to others with smiles, eye contact, compliments, and everyday conversation. The more you do this, the easier it becomes. Push yourself! Practice!

Step 3

When you meet some friends "try it out." Ask yourself if these individuals are right for you. Are they the types of people your family would want you to be with. Remember that people who pressure you into doing "bad" stuff don't care about you! They care about their own power trip. Real power comes from inside, from being sure of yourself, even if that sets you apart from the crowd. If a situation comes up and there's pressure to do something you don't want to do, be confident. At some point you'll get respect for being strong and independent. When the pressure is subtle – when "everybody's doing it" – ask yourself, "Do I want to be everybody, or do I want to be somebody?"

Step 4

Work on the qualities of being a good friend. Are you sensitive to others' feelings? Are you trustworthy? Are you patient? Do you think before you act?

Step 5

If the model isn't working, take a time out and begin again.

Teachers, Counselors & Social Workers

Simple Refusal Skills

Peer pressure has a tremendous amount of power over our students. Students not only need to practice nonverbal assertiveness skills, but they also need to practice some assertive verbal skills, so that when it is necessary to refuse participation they will have some memorized statements to use.

Below are six suggestions on how to say "NO." Have students identify the phrases that match their age and style and have them practice the phrases at home in the privacy of their own space. Tell them to practice saying the phrases with an assertive tone (not too loud and not too soft), and to stand tall. Don't get into an argument. Just say "NO" and walk AWAY!

Simple Refusal Skills:

Just say, "No" - *"Not for me."*

Act shocked – *"You're taking a chance at getting arrested."*

Laugh it off - *"No thanks. I've got enough problems."*

Make an excuse – *"Can't. I need to keep my mind and body in shape for football."*

Offer a better idea – *"That is not right for me. Let's go play ball."*

Turn the tables – If someone refuses to take no for an answer, put the pressure on the other person. *"What's the matter? Are you afraid to stand up for what is right?"*

Adapted from Mathis, T. and Smith-Rex, S. (2002). *Getting your life on track: a female teen's guide to saying no to sex.* Minn. MN: Educational Media.

Have the students come up with several other statements that could fit the six categories listed above. List them on the following page – Memorize Assertive Phrases – and take them home for practice. Remind students to look directly in a mirror and assertively use a proper tone.

© YouthLight, Inc.

Reproducible Worksheet

Memorize Assertive Phrases

Write a statement of your own for each of the Simple Refusal Skills' examples. Take the sheet home, memorize, and practice your statements. Remember to look directly in a mirror and assertively use a proper tone.

Just say, "No" - _____
_____

Act shocked - _____
_____

Laugh it off - _____
_____

Make an excuse - _____
_____

Offer a better idea - _____
_____

Turn the tables - _____
_____

Samantha St. Aubin

Teachers, Counselors & Social Workers

Dream and Reflect!!

When a person gets into the habit of setting goals, reflecting upon personal effort, and dreaming about the future, it usually motivates individuals to push themselves.

Using maps or a globe, talk about places one would like to visit. Revisit the long-term goals that students selected in the Setting Goals in My Life Worksheet (page 50). Emphasize that anything worth having in life requires hard work, a positive attitude, and a sense of hope.

Ask students to set aside a few minutes each day to close their eyes and picture themselves achieving the goal or visiting the place. The more hopeful, knowledgeable, and determined one becomes, the more obvious it is to most individuals that a good attitude and hard work are vitally important.

Teachers, Counselors & Social Workers

Gardner's Multiple Intelligence Theory

Dr. Howard Gardner, from Harvard University, has done extensive research on the theory that there are at least eight important types of intelligence. The reason it is important for students, parents, and educators to support the Gardner Theory is that a strong self-esteem is largely based on the belief that all individuals are talented and valued in some area of their intellectual being (Gardner, 1983).

Make an overlay of the illustration below and discuss the varied intelligences with the students.

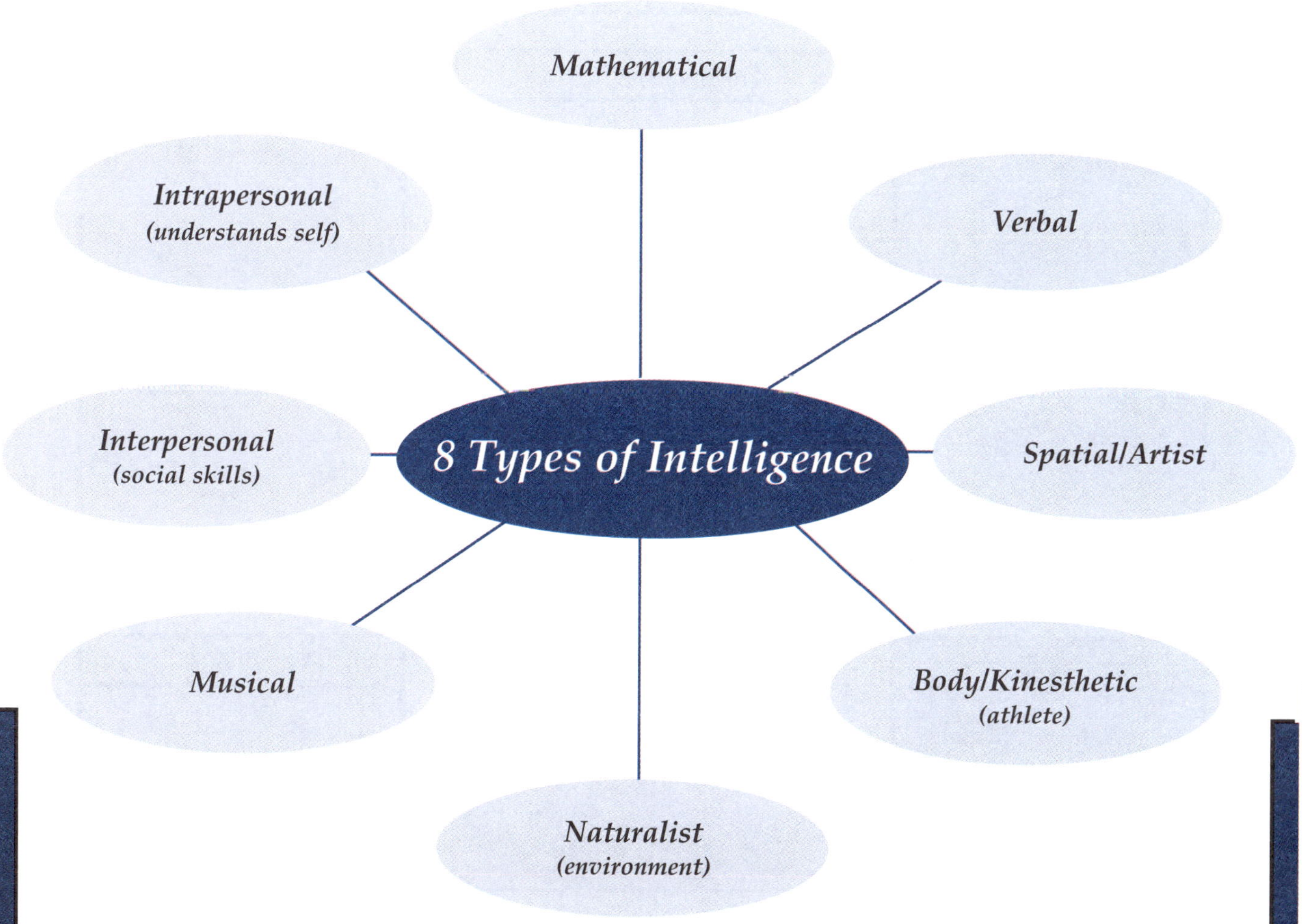

8 Types of Intelligence
- Mathematical
- Verbal
- Spatial/Artist
- Body/Kinesthetic (athlete)
- Naturalist (environment)
- Musical
- Interpersonal (social skills)
- Intrapersonal (understands self)

Adapted from Gardner (1983)

67

Reproducible Worksheet

Feeling and Believing You Are Good *At Something!*

Everyone can be and needs to be good at something! Possessing credible skills allows individuals to participate in and sometimes lead activities which builds a sense of self-worth.

After reviewing the Gardner Model, be specific and list interests and skills which you have. You do not have to be great at something, just good!

Clubs I Belong To:	Community Interests:	Church Interests:

Outdoor Interests:	Athletic Interests:	Music Interests:

Art Interests:	Drama Interests:	Dance Interests:

Things I Collect:	Subjects I Would Like To Learn More About:	My Perfect Vacation:

Become a valuable resource to your school by making a classroom presentation to share your area of interest.

© YouthLight, Inc.

Reproducible Worksheet

Finding a Cause You Believe In

Revisit once again the Gardner Multiple Intelligence Theory (page 67), but this time evaluate your strengths and interests and how they relate to personal, local, or national causes. It is very possible for young people to make a BIG difference in other peoples' lives by demonstrating a passion and a desire to work hard.

On the blank spaces below, write project causes you believe you would like to learn more about. Use the internet to research the wide range of possibilities.

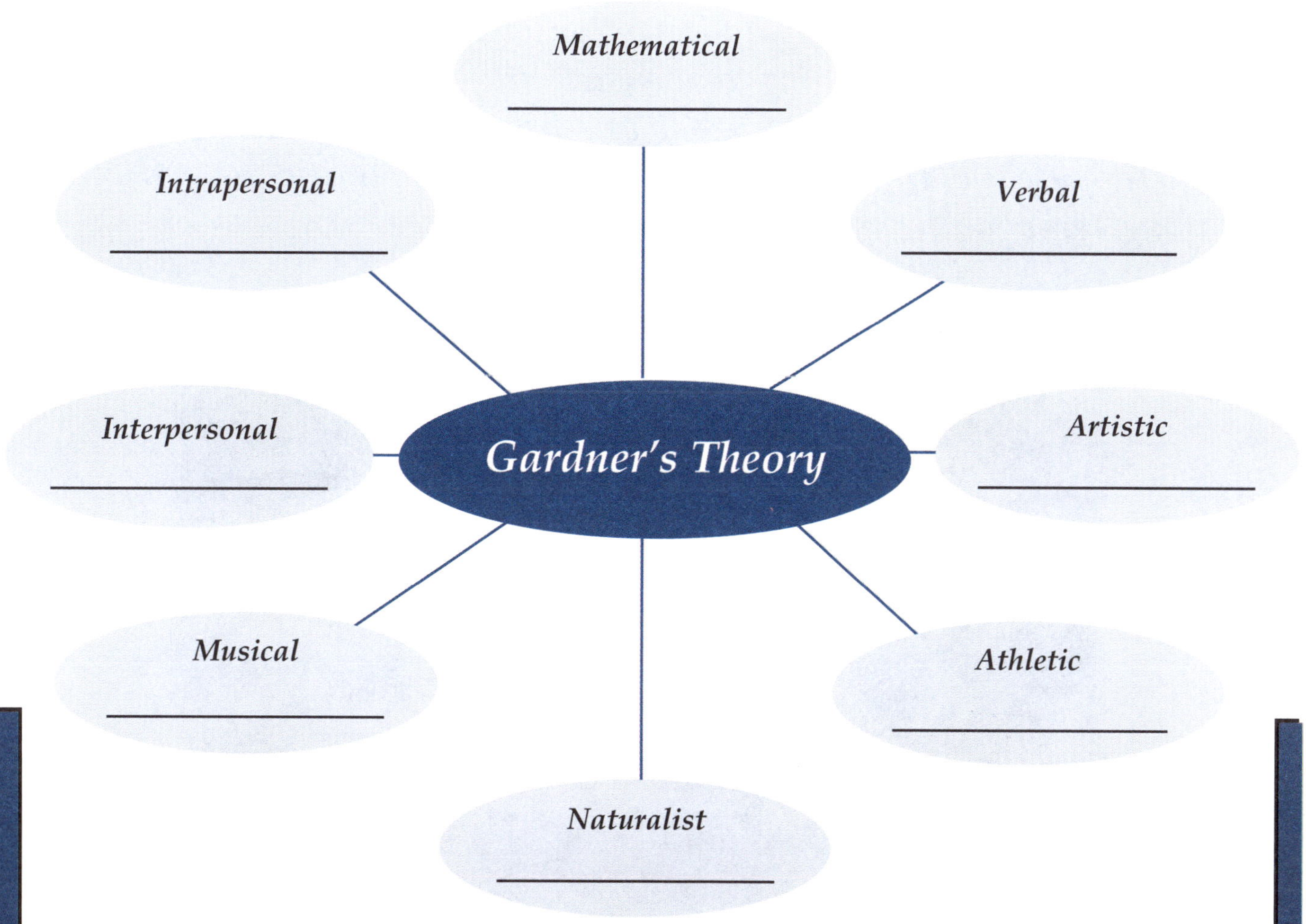

- Mathematical _____
- Verbal _____
- Artistic _____
- Athletic _____
- Naturalist _____
- Musical _____
- Interpersonal _____
- Intrapersonal _____

Gardner's Theory

Teachers, Counselors & Social Workers

Habit Forming
Acts of Kindness

Empathy is defined as identifying and understanding another person's situation or feeling (American Heritage Dictionary). Getting ahead in life is a matter of both hard work and a lot of luck! Keeping that thought in mind can help individuals to be less self–centered and to want to reach out to others through their actions and their pleasant manners. Being kind and considerate are qualities that bring most people a lot of pleasure, satisfaction, and happiness.

Ask students to read and consider the benefits of the examples on the Habit Forming Acts of Kindness Reproducible Worksheet (page 71). After reflecting on the values, ask students to list three behaviors they are going to consistently display immediately (short-term goals) and at least one behavior they are going to participate in at their school, church, community, or nation (long-term goal).

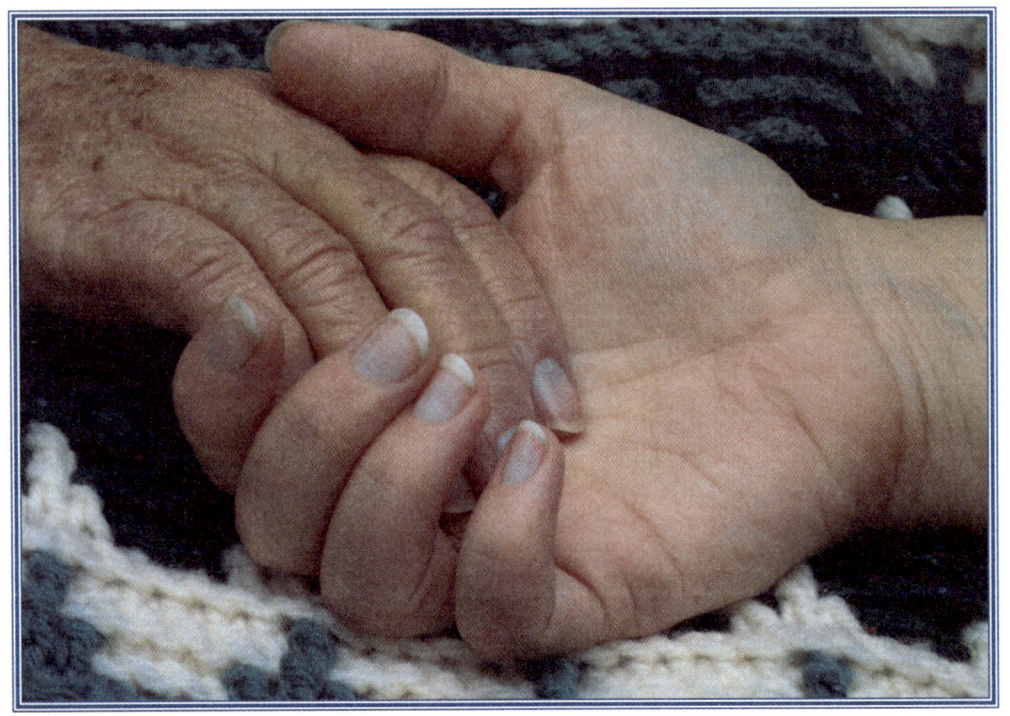

© YouthLight, Inc.

Reproducible Worksheet

Habit Forming
Acts of Kindness

After reflecting on the following acts of kindness, list three behaviors you will consistently display immediately (short-term goals) and at least one behavior you will participate in at your school, church, community, or nation (long-term goal).

Short-Term:

- Smile at a lot of people each day.
- Hold the door for someone.
- Let a person move ahead of you in a line.
- Give another person your seat.
- Consistently ask your family what you can do to help.
- Tell your family members that you love them.
- Eliminate sarcasm from the tone of your voice.

Long-Term:

- Participate in a school project which benefits others.
- Call up "Habitat For Humanity" and join in!
- Ask your minister how to best use your time to help a member of your congregation.
- Seek out an elderly neighbor who could use some help.
- Get involved in a national project, such as "Keep America Beautiful."
- Write editorials to encourage your classmates to see the importance and personal satisfaction that comes from extending acts of kindness.

© YouthLight, Inc.

Your Short-Term Goals

_____
_____
_____

Your Long-Term Goals

_____
_____
_____

For Parents

Part III

Practical Ideas To Help Your Child Grow Into A Happier Adult

For Parents

Modeling - The Dance of Parenthood

Parents are instrumental in providing adult modeling for their children. How we react to life's challenges is a powerful influence. We don't have to be perfect, but we do need to be aware - aware that our choices, our behaviors, and our attitudes are being observed.

It's a bit ironic, but the responsibility of parenting often makes the parent a healthier, happier adult. How many parents have quit smoking, swearing, drinking, etc., because they were concerned about the effects of their behavior on their child? Parents and their children are irrevocably linked in the dance of life – sometimes we lead, sometimes they lead. At times it is a slow dance with intimacy and close coordination. Other times, the beat is erratic, the tunes indistinguishable, and we don't seem to be in the same room- let alone moving as one. But, we are always aware of the other, where they are, where they aren't, what they are doing.

When you think about your child and his or her happiness – think about your own level of happiness. How can you improve upon it? How can you show those around you that you have accepted responsibility for improving it? And, most importantly, how can your dance partner benefit from your example and from your greater experience on the dance floor of life.

© YouthLight, Inc.

For Parents

Over Structuring Childhood

How much structure is good for children and adolescents? For that matter, how much is good for adults? The easy answer is to say that it depends upon the child or adult. Like most easy answers, this one doesn't offer much direction to parents who are concerned about the right balance for their particular child.

Over the past 20 years the amount of time children ages nine to twelve spend participating in structured sports has increased by 35%, according to a study conducted at the University of Maryland (Time, 1/17/05, p.A65). That, coupled with school attendance, school work, music, art, clubs, etc. has created, for some, a childhood that is as heavily booked and scheduled as any ambitious, overworked adult.

Time, time to dream (daydream?), create, experiment, rest, and explore is all too often sacrificed in an attempt to fill childhood with the synonyms of adult life. Many adults look back at their fondest memories of childhood as the "lazy days of summer," the vacation, the camping trip with little structure, or the informal times with friends when life was discussed and imagined without adults or programming.

Look for the signs that may mean your child needs "down time." They are similar to the ones that adults exhibit when overextended: irritability, confusion about schedules, tiredness, resentment. If you see these signs, consider taking some time to "allow" for your child to have an entire day or block of time with little structure. You might suggest that you, too, need a break and maybe you could go for a walk or a hike. If time allows, a trip to no particular destination may free up time – and the imagination. And, then there is the option to do "nothing." Kick back, listen to your favorite music, read, whatever the mood of the moment suggests.

Staying busy is fine. It is the way we accomplish much in our lives. It is not, however, the only approach to happiness. Just as some adults discover that their lives have become too structured, children may need the insight from an adult to help them strike a balance that addresses their particular need for solitude, introspection, or constructive idleness.

© YouthLight, Inc.

For Parents
Helping Your Child Deal With Rejection

Sporadic doses of negative experiences are inevitable in life and can actually be valuable. It is through stressful events or occasional rejection that people learn to bounce back from unpleasant emotions. This ability is often referred to as resiliency.

Parents have deep-seated impulses to jump in and protect their children from rejection. It is hard to forget the first time your child was turned down for something he or she reeeally wanted! However, it is important to remind yourself that setbacks can help your child develop the resilience he or she will need to handle a world that isn't always fair or supportive.

Consider demonstrating the following behaviors when your child feels rejected or sad.

1. *Initially it is OK to let your child grieve. Your child may need a little time to be alone, weep, or just receive a hug.*
2. *Once your child has calmed down, share a story about a time when you were disappointed. (See Parental Storytelling - pg 76).*
3. *Ask your child to give you a possible reason for not being selected or accepted. Accept her answer as one possibility, then ask her what other reasons there might be. When you introduce alternatives scenarios, your child can see that the rejection may not be so personal.*
4. *Discuss alternative ways to use personal time. It is helpful to share Gardner's Intelligence Theory - (pg 67).*
5. *Read Part I of this book with your child. Emphasize that much of one's happiness can be controlled.*
6. *Guide your child to put "set backs" into perspective. When your child discovers personal strengths and understands how to feel some control over his personal happiness, he develops a base that can't be shaken by day-to-day setbacks. (See Front Burner - Back Burner Strategy - pg 49).*
7. *Monitor your own disappointment and anger regarding your child's rejection. If a parent overreacts, you may be over identifying with your child.*
8. *Sometimes it is a good idea to discuss your concerns with a sensitive teacher, counselor, or coach. (See Reach Out & Control Isolation - pg 62).*
9. *Remember, you want to help your child to deal with rejection without letting the incident prevent him from taking risks in the future!*

© YouthLight, Inc.

For Parents
Parental Storytelling

It is hard to overstate the power of storytelling. All of us remember and are more likely to relate to the messages in a well-told story. Hollywood and sophisticated communicators of all kinds have learned this lesson well.

Parents can not only make powerful and lasting impressions upon their children through stories; but, by personalizing those stories, they can also share the fact that they, and all adults, struggled at times while growing up. Your stories can emphasize poor choices or mistakes that you made while growing up and the learning that took place as you dealt with the consequences. Among other things, these stories can help children realize that you don't expect perfection, but that you do expect continual growth and an effort to improve.

Deep down, children want to please their parents. They also are fascinated by the realization that these people, whom they have only known as adults, were once children. Introduce them to the child you were (and to some extent, still are) and help your child see you as not only someone who stands beside them, but as someone who has traveled some of their road before them.

For Parents

Stick to Commitments

Today, with children often being over committed with sports, private lessons, and school clubs, parents have an important job to help their children select those activities they are most committed to. Once the selection is made, it is almost always important for parents to encourage and insist that their child stick to their commitments.

Children build resiliency by learning that there are "ups and downs" with all jobs and activities. Parents should try to role model this skill through their own coping skills. The older one becomes the more important it is to be able to stick with something. If your child is repeatedly bailing out, ask yourself these questions:

1. Did I have a thorough conversation with my child regarding his loss of interest?

2. Does my child seem to have fear and if so, is it rational? (See "What Are Rational and Irrational Fears," pg 54)

3. Is my child burnt out or bored? If so, maybe there is a need to cut back or bring about a change. This, however, should never be a common response. If it is needed, carefully make the change and make it clear that there will be a commitment to the new schedule or activity.

4. Does my child expect perfection? Help your child understand that the only way to improve is to stay in the game. Quitting in "mid stream" should not be an option.

5. Am I trying to push my interests and dreams too hard on my child? Remember that your child is unique and must develop his or her own interests in life. There may be some overlap with the areas in life that interest you; but there may be no connection. Pushing too hard can guarantee the latter.

© YouthLight, Inc.

For Parents
Components to a Healthy Self-Esteem

By definition, self-esteem refers to satisfaction with oneself. Having a healthy self-esteem places a child in a much less vulnerable position to dislike school and to have difficulty setting short-term or long-term goals. (See Setting Goals In My Life - pg 50).

Individuals with a healthy self-esteem often have a feeling of peace and well-being. These are individuals who are more able to make better choices, be true friends, and feel a sense of happiness.

According to educational literature from the American Medical Association, there are five important components to a healthy self-esteem (Roth & Clifton, 2004). Ask yourself if you are helping your child achieve the following feelings:

A Feeling of Security
~at home, school, and neighborhood~

A Positive Identity
~feeling noticed for one's strengths and for doing what is expected~

A Feeling of Belonging
~emotional goals have been identified~

A Sense of Purpose
~meaningful goals have been identified~

A Feeling of Competence
~being good at something one enjoys~

All of the above feelings are discussed in Part I.

© YouthLight, Inc.

For Parents

10 Things Parents Can Do to Help Children Develop a Healthy Self-Esteem

1. Set and communicate high expectations.

2. Give caring and insightful feedback.

3. Encourage children to be involved in at least one school or community group.

4. Help children to achieve in something they choose.

5. Set up opportunities for children to give of themselves to others.

6. Practice good decision-making skills and independent work habits. Monitor too much TV, computer, and phone use.

7. Establish a personal faith and respect in something greater then oneself.

8. Provide a warm, inviting atmosphere.

9. Aggressive behavior is not considered acceptable. Watch the use of sarcasm and negativism.

10. Monitor children's whereabouts!

Adapted from Smith-Rex, S.& Rex, J. (2005).
101 Creative Strategies For Reaching Unmotivated Student Learners. Chapin, SC: Youthlight.

© YouthLight, Inc.

For Parents

The Natural World

Our genetic make-up connects us all to the natural world around us. The tallest skyscrapers in the world have real or imitation plants, paintings of natural scenes, etc. No matter what man builds, he feels a need to ensure that a connection to nature is included. How each of us chooses to perceive and enjoy the natural world around us is largely shaped during childhood.

A forest that appears dark and forbidding to one person, is a sought after refuge for sports, observation, or reflection by another. A mountain range that is viewed as a barren, cold, uninviting barrier to progress by one person, is viewed as a breathtakingly beautiful invitation to climb, hike, ski, camp and explore by another. Often, our perceptions of the natural world and our place in it are formed during our childhood.

As our world becomes more urbanized, many seek this sense of connection to the natural world wherever they are able to find it; parks, zoos, films, and books are often good ways to introduce children to animals, plants, and the environments they live in.

Certainly children and adults can be happy and content within urban settings, and rural residents can be unhappy and discontented. It isn't about where you live that seems to matter, it's your understanding of, and your appreciation for, your place in the amazing system that supports life on our planet. Try to help your child gain that understanding and appreciation. It will serve them well as they live their lives within that system.

© YouthLight, Inc.

For Parents

Personal Beliefs
and Spirituality

Research supports the fact that people who belong to an organized religious group, or who adhere to a particular formal set of beliefs regarding their "inner being" and its relationship to the universe around them, are more likely to rate themselves at a higher level of happiness then those without such beliefs (Time, 1/17/05, p.A46). These beliefs can provide comfort and predictability throughout life's storms and tribulations. They can also set boundaries and limits that may help reduce a number of choices/temptations.

The freedom we have in America to believe, or not to believe, in a particular religion is one of our most important freedoms. There is evidence, however, that believing in something, other than ourselves, is extremely comforting to a large percentage of Americans.

What a parent does with this information is an intensely personal decision. Some parents are comfortable enough in their own beliefs to actively advocate their adoption for their child. Other parents attempt to expose their children to a variety of faiths and beliefs in the hope that the child will exercise his or her right to choose at an appropriate age. Still others take a passive approach and allow their child to decide if, as a child or as an adult, they wish to pursue and adopt a particular religion or faith.

In the final analysis it will ultimately be up to your child to decide, as an adult, whether to adopt a set of beliefs that may assist him or her in understanding, and coping, with life. What role, if any, you decide to play in that process will, in all probability, be largely decided by your own particular set of beliefs.

© YouthLight, Inc.

For Parents
Knowing Your Family History and Ethnic Heritage

When the best selling novel and movie "Roots" came out a few decades ago, some professed surprise at what a powerful impact it had on so many Americans, and especially upon African Americans. Its influence, however, is partially understood by recognizing that, for many, it was the first time they had been given the opportunity to view their past, their heritage.

All of us, sooner or later, want to know where we came from and who were the people we are genetically connected to? Part of this desire is the normal curiosity most of us have about our physical inheritances (where did I get this nose, these eyes, this disposition?). But, knowing about our family, our ancestors, can also bring a sense of pride; a sense of belonging to a particular continuum of humanity with whom we share a bond that bridges time.

While many families have limited information regarding their family history, almost all have some. Even if it is only the last generation (grandparents) or this generation (aunts, uncles, cousins) make sure your child knows about these people and how they are related. When possible, help them to get to know them, or at least to talk to them by telephone or through letters.

Often, young children or adolescents will appear to have little interest in family history or ethnic heritage, but they absorb more than may be apparent. The sense of belonging, even the sense of pride, may not be easily apparent; but it will be there and it will be called upon, when needed.

© YouthLight, Inc.

For Parents
Be A Model For *Your Children!*

Below are listed 12 thoughts regarding parental behavior. Read each one and evaluate yourself. Work on improving in some of these areas, in order to help your children more smoothly make the inevitable transition into adulthood. Remember that most people need structure and predictability in their lives. Part I of this book stresses to the child the importance of controlling their own behavior. This works for parents as well.

Don't do things your child can do for himself/herself.

Don't spoil your child. Your child should not have everything he/she asks for.

Don't be afraid to be firm but fair.

Don't correct your child harshly in front of others. A person notices more if you talk quietly in a private place.

Don't always demand explanations for wrong behavior.

Don't always preach to your child. You'd be surprised how well he/she knows right from wrong.

Don't use force. It teaches your child that power is all that counts.

Don't be inconsistent. That confuses your child and makes him try harder to get away with poor choices.

Don't make promises you are not going to keep.

Don't let "bad habits" get a lot of your attention. It may encourage your child to continue them.

Don't try to protect your child from due consequences. Your child needs to learn from their own experiences.

Don't let your fears arouse their anxiety. Your child will become more afraid of failing.

© YouthLight, Inc.

For Parents
Coaching Your Child's
Health Habits

Probably the most common toast on earth is to another's good health. Good health and happiness have a high correlation among most populations of people. We can't choose our genetics, but we can, and do, choose our life styles. It's those choices and the habitual decisions around them that can help a person to lead a healthier, and happier, life.

A good coach pays close attention to the health habits of his or her athletes. What they eat, how much exercise they get, how much sleep they receive, whether or not they are using hazardous substances (smoking, alcohol, drugs, etc.) are all monitored by conscientious coaches, because they know that poor decisions in these areas will lead to poor performance. And while athletic competition can be a valuable experience for players and fans alike; its significance pales when compared to the "event" we are preparing our child for – the life-long event called "life." Surely, we can be as diligent as any good coach in helping our child learn to eat healthy foods, exercise regularly, sleep at least eight hours per day and to resist substances that will harm his or her body.

It is easier to feel happy when your physical being feels good. As with so many things in parenting (and coaching), modeling the behaviors you value will help you convince others of their value. So, think of your task as being similar to the coach preparing his player for the big game – actually, the biggest game of all!!

© YouthLight, Inc.

For Parents

Knowing When To Feel
Pride Versus Gratitude

I once heard a very publicly and visibly proud man, who had been blessed with many advantages throughout his life, described quite critically by another. The critic proclaimed, "There is someone who was born on third base, but thinks he's hit a triple." I don't know if the criticism was in this case justified; but it points out the importance of the need to help our children understand when it is justified to feel pride and when it is necessary to feel gratitude.

The sense of accomplishment is an important contributor to feelings of contentment and happiness. Often, the more difficult the accomplishment, the greater the level of satisfaction.

It is, however, important to also know how to recognize and be grateful for the physical attributes, the mental abilities and the familial resources that we have been given. Sometimes the "luck of the draw" is positive and sometimes it is negative. What really matters most, of course, is what we do with the cards we are dealt in life.

All of us have "cards" we should be grateful for. Parents can help their child take an assessment of the good things they possess in life. You can also help them recognize what they have accomplished with the cards dealt them – what they should justifiably be proud of. (See "Front Burner - Back Burner Strategy" - pg 49 and "Feeling & Believing You Are Good At Something" - pg 68).

Nurturing these skills: how to recognize and appreciate our blessings, and how to recognize and derive pleasure from our accomplishments, can be important contributors to happiness. Helping your child learn the importance of gratitude and the satisfaction of justifiable pride will strengthen their self-awareness, self-confidence, and empathy for others.

© YouthLight, Inc.

For Parents

Learning to Aim Before We Fire!

Too often, parents say things in anger or frustration that they wish they could take back or rephrase. Not only does this "shooting from the lip" often cause unnecessary pain, alienation and resentment; but it also provides a poor model for children as they learn how to react to conflict and disagreement. Regret is a powerful, negative emotion in life. Some regret is inevitable in life, but people who consistently regret their responses to others experience a roller coaster of emotions that betray their attempts at happiness.

An important skill to teach to our children is the ability to think before we speak and to aim before we fire; a misdirected phrase, just like a misdirected bullet, can do irreparable harm. There are different tactics that can help with acquiring this ability. Some people are able to mentally play a tape or film of their preferred response (almost like an instant "audition") before they decide if it is an appropriate option. Learning to wait until they have "reviewed" their responses allows these people to avoid much of the regret that more spontaneous people must endure.

Another strategy is to learn to pause before you respond. This gives you more time to consider alternative responses. It also often helps create more interest in, and attention to, your ultimate response.

Still another option is to say nothing when you are unsure of the best response. Often silence, or walking away, is the best immediate response. This often allows both parties to calm down and resist a cycle of inappropriate or escalating responses. You can always make your statement later – perhaps more eloquently and calmly.

An important skill that enables us to reduce regret in our lives is the ability to choose responses to conflict that we can live with. Learning to aim our verbal weapons before we pull the trigger is critical for parents, and our children, as we interact with those around us.

© YouthLight, Inc.

For Parents
Envisioning Our Futures

Virtually every parent is concerned about their child's future. We think about it and, sometimes, we talk about it; but often we don't truly discuss it with our children. This may be part of the reason why many adults, especially young adults, report that they rarely think about, or plan for, their futures.

While part of the search for happiness is learning about and accepting what can and cannot be controlled in life; generally, people who set realistic goals and make plans to achieve them report higher-levels of contentment and achievement than those who see the future as something that need not be examined, nor envisioned.

Helping children think about, and envision, their future takes time, patience and some creativity. The single most important ingredient is time. Time for the parent and child to talk and listen to each other. One desired atmosphere is one in which there is an unhurried, confidential, and unstructured exploration of "what ifs." In such an atmosphere, both the adult and the child can investigate the feasibility and possibility of a range of options for their individual, and common, futures. Topics such as the relative merits of instant gratification versus delayed gratification and the wisdom of setting ambitious, versus more realistic, goals can be thoroughly discussed and examined.

Parents who take the time to create appropriate environments to discuss the future with their child help provide that child with a powerful tool to assist them as they chart their course in life. The winds and currents of life will inevitably alter their chosen courses; but to have no chart or destination in mind sadly ensures that the satisfaction of "staying on course", as well as envisioning and hailing distant landfalls, will not be a part of their experience.

Helpful Strategies:
Front Burner - Back Burner Strategy - pg 49
Setting Goals In My Life - pg 50
Dream & Reflect - pg 66

© YouthLight, Inc.

For Parents

The Gift of Giving

Helping your child experience the joys of giving – the giving of time and the giving of possessions to benefit others – should rank highly on every parent's list of responsibilities. As we grow older, we often learn that the satisfaction and sense of fulfillment that comes from helping another or supporting a worthwhile cause rank among the highest pleasures in life. Many of the happiest people on Earth are those who give the most of themselves to others and to causes that benefit others. A child who is able to experience the joys of giving is indeed fortunate and is likely to become an adult who seeks out such opportunities throughout their lifetime.

The opportunities for childhood giving and volunteering may need to be identified and facilitated by a parent or another adult. Schools, churches, synagogues, and mosques, offer a variety of options. Charitable organizations and not-for-profit organizations provide numerous events and programs. The local evening news almost always has, unfortunately, a number of individuals and families who are in need of assistance. And, individual observations and local word of mouth can usually identify those in temporary, or more lasting, need.

The point here is that whether it is picking up litter, fixing up and giving away toys, donating a portion of one's allowance, or helping with a worthwhile fundraising event; your child deserves the opportunity to experience the gift of giving. A gift that can help provide purpose, satisfaction, and happiness in their life.

© YouthLight, Inc.

For Parents
Discovering Your
Optimum Environment

All of us have sensory inclinations that can assist us as we attempt to relax, create, or feel a heightened sense of comfort and enjoyment. A type of music, a particular combination of colors, a favorite fragrance, certain examples of art, or a preferred degree of light or darkness are examples of sensory choices that can affect our emotions and sense of well-being. While all of us react to one degree or another to the presence or absence of such factors in our environment, we don't often enough think about the choices we do have and their impact upon us.

While the saying, "A man's home is his castle" doesn't necessarily pertain to a child, there can be a room or a space that he or she can identify with and take particular responsibility for. The way that designated area looks and "feels" can become the responsibility of your child. Guidelines and guidance in terms of cost and limits should be explained, but the license to create should be encouraged. Another condition for this creative license should be that visitors must be not only allowed, but welcomed. They must understand that they should expect to explain, but never to defend, their choices.

Someday, your child will be making these choices again as they move into an apartment, a home, and/or an office. Now is the time to begin experimenting with, and learning about, the choices that make their personal environment both nurturing and comforting.

© YouthLight, Inc.

For Parents
Learning to Avoid "Jerks"

All of us know, or have known, individuals whose mere presence in a room, or within a group, creates an atmospheric change. In their case, it is never a change for the better. Heightened anxiety, negativity and/or confrontation seems to follow them wherever they go. Their ability to rain on a good conversation, party, dinner or social event is legendary. We sometimes even joke about these people by saying things like, "He doesn't get ulcers, he gives them," or "She doesn't have nervous breakdowns, she causes them."

The negative effects inflicted upon the lives of others by these people are, however, no laughing matter. The only thing worse than being one of these people, is to feel constrained to be around them. Whether a relative, neighbor, co-worker, or classmate, they can have a devastating effect on one's level of happiness.

It is important for all of us to learn how to identify these people in our lives, assess our options to eliminate or minimize our contact with them, and then to politely and effectively implement our best strategic option for eliminating or diminishing their negative effects on our lives.

Help your child recognize such people, if they exist in your child's life, and discuss the various options available to eliminate, or minimize, the negative effects of that person. The severity may range from bullying to distracting and counterproductive personality traits; but children, and adults, need to learn how to exercise control and implement choices when confronted by such personalities. Life is too short, at any age, to put up with "jerks!"

Helpful Strategies:
The Effects of Negative Thinking - pg 48
What are Rational and Irrational Fears - pg 54
Evaluate Your Anxiety - pg 55
The Friendship Model - pg 57
Selecting the Right Friends - pg 63
Simple Refusal Skills - pg 64

© YouthLight, Inc.

For Parents
Finding the Humor In Life

Research shows that the physical act of laughter has measurable health benefits. We also know that a sense of humor is one of the most highly ranked human attributes listed when people are surveyed about what is an important characteristic in a friend or spouse. Finally, experience has shown us that a leader who can exhibit (or fake) self-deprecating humor has a very good chance of enhancing his popularity among followers.

Life can be serious – deadly serious, but there appears to be an innate human need to "lighter up" our inevitable heavy burdens, whenever possible, with the wondrous tonic called humor. People who can express humor are popular and people who can find it in their lives seem to have an inherent advantage over those who can't. The serious "Scrooges" of the world often seem to live shorter, lonelier and darker lives.

It is important for parents to attempt to not take themselves (and their parenting) too seriously, as they interact with their children. Help your child to see both the irony and the humor in life that almost always exists, everyday, in the world around us. Look for opportunities to laugh, especially at yourself (your kid(s) will love it), as you share your experiences with one another.

It may not be possible to instill the gifts of the humorist in another, but we can all learn to appreciate and savor the inherent laughter that is all around us, and in us, as we live our lives.

© YouthLight, Inc.

For Parents
Avoiding an Unexamined Life!

The popular unattributed quotation that, "No one on their deathbed ever wished they had spent more time at work," may not always have been the case (what if someone truly loved their work?), but it captures the pathos of individuals who mindlessly expend their precious and limited days in pursuits that they ultimately and tragically regret. It's almost as if they were too busy all those years to take the time to ask themselves about what matters most in life, to them. It's important to live life fully, but it is also important to give some thought to and even some deliberation to an examination of what "fully" means to each of us.

Childhood, and adolescence, is not too early to have discussions about what makes one happy, and why. Children know when they're happy and sad, but they may not have given much thought to causes and effects or whether recurring patterns of choices are contributing to how they feel. If your child can begin to realize that they can have some real control over how they feel about life, and themselves, you will have given them an insight more valuable then any inheritance. An unexamined life increases the probability that we will never begin to understand who we are, what matters most to us, and how our choices in life can contribute to our level of happiness.

Helpful Strategies:
Chart Your Feelings - pg 47
Front Burner - Back Burner Strategy - pg 49
Dream and Reflect - pg 66
Habit Forming Acts of Kindness - pg 70

© YouthLight, Inc.

Final Thought on "The Pursuit of Happiness"

Whether you find yourself using this book as a parent, a teacher, a counselor, or other concerned professional, to help adolescents find and enhance their pursuit of happiness, thank you. Thank you for your motivation to help them, and all of us!

References

Alaoui-Ismaieli, O., O. Robin, H. Rada, A. Dittmar, and E. Vernet-Maury. 1997. "Basic Emotions Evoked by Odorants." Physiology and Behavior 62:713.

Barofsky, I. and A. Rowan. 1998. "Models for Measuring Quality of Life: Implications for Human-Animal Interaction Research." In Companion Animals in Human Health. Thousand Oaks, CA:Sage.

Castillo, S., Mathis, T., and Smith-Rex, S. 2000. "Getting Face to Face with Your Fears: A Kid's Guide to Understanding and Coping with Fears and Phobias." Minneapolis, MN: Educational Media.

Crist-Houran, M. 1996. "Efficacy of Volunteerism." Psychological Reports 79:736.

Diener, E. and C. Diener. 1996. "Most People Are Happy." Psychological Science 7:181.

Fontane, P. 1996. "Exercise, Fitness, and Feeling Well." American Behavior Scientist 39:288.

Frank, K. and Smith-Rex, S. 1994. "Getting A Grip On ADD: A Kid's Guide to Understanding and Coping with Attention Disorders." The Friendship Model- Minneapolis, MN: Educational Media Corporation.

Frank, K. and Smith-Rex, S. 1995. "Getting a Life of Your Own: A Kid's Guide to Understanding and Coping with Family Alcoholism." Minneapolis, MN: Educational Media Corporation.

Frank, K. and Smith-Rex, S. 1996. "Getting Over the Blues: A Kid's Guide to Understanding and Coping with Unpleasant Feelings and Depression." Minneapolis, MN: Educational Media Corporation.

Gardner, H. 1983. Frames of Mind. New York: Basic Books.

Garrett, R. 1996. "Wisdom as the Key to a Better World." In Contemporary Issues in Behavior Therapy. New York: Plenum.

Gerwood, J., M. LeBlanc, N. Piazza. 1998. "The Purpose in Life Test and Religious Denomination." Journal of Clinical Psychology 54:49.

Hakanen, E. 1995. "Emotional Use of Music by African American Adolescents." Howard Journal of Communications 5:124.

Heatey, K. and D. Thombs. 1997. "Fruit-Vegetable Consumption Self-Efficacy in Youth." American Journal of Health Behavior 21:172.

Lundqvist, L. and U. Dimberg. 1995. "Facial Expressions Are Contagious." Journal of Psychophysiology 9:203.

Lykken, D. and A. Tellegen. 1996. "Happiness Is a Stochastic Phenomenon." Psychological Science 7:186.

Lyubomirsky, S. 1994. "Hedonistic Consequences of Social Comparison: Implications for Enduring Happiness and Transient Mood." Ph.D diss., Stanford University, Palo Alto, California.

References

Magen, Z., M. Birenbaum, and D. Pery. 1996. "Experiencing Joy and Sorrow." *International Forum for Logotherapy* 19:45.

Mathis, T. and Smith-Rex, S. 2002. "Getting Your Life on Track: A Female Teen's Guide to Saying No to Sex." Minneapolis, MN: Educational Media.

Mathis, T. and Smith-Rex, S. 2001. "Getting Ahead: Strategies to Motivate and Assist Students with Classroom Learning." Minneapolis, MN: Educational Media.

Mookherjee, H. 1997. "Perception of Well-Being Among Older Persons in Nonmetropolitan America." *Perceptual and Motor Skills* 85:943.

Murray, C., and M.J. Peacock. 1996. "A Model-Free Approach to the Study of Subjective Well-Being." In *Mental Health in Black America*. Thousand Oaks, Cal:Sage.

Neto, F. 1995. "Predictors of Satisfaction with Life." *Social Indicators Research* 35:93.

Niven, D. 2000. "The 100 Simple Secrets Of Happy People." New York, NY: Harper Collins Publishers.

Pilcher, J. and E. Ott. 1998. "The Relationship Between Sleep and Measures of Health and Well-Being in College Students: A Repeated Measures Approach." *Behavioral Medicine* 23:170.

Rath, T. and D., Clifton 2004. "How Full Is Your Bucket." New York, NY: Gallup Press.

Seligman, M. 2002. "Authentic Happiness." New York, NY: Gallup Press.

Shank, M. and F. Beasley. 1998. "Fan or Fanatic: Refining a Measure of Sports Involvement." *Journal of Sport Behavior* 21:435.

Smith, S J. and Walter, G. Four Steps To Making Friends. Rock Hill, SC. Winthrop University.

Smith-Rex, S. and Rex, J. 2005. "101 Creative Strategies for Reaching Unmotivated Student Learners." Chapin, SC: Youthlight.

Time Magazine, Jan.17, 2005. "The New Science of Happiness." A3-A68.